AMERICA'S CONFRONTATION WITH REVOLUTIONARY CHANGE IN THE MIDDLE EAST, 1948–83

By the same author

SUPREMACY AND OIL: Iraq, Turkey and the Anglo–American World
Order, 1918–1930

America's Confrontation with Revolutionary Change in the Middle East, 1948–83

DISCARDED

William Stivers

Director, International Relations Graduate Program
University of Southern California, Frankfurt

St. Martin's Press   New York

First published in the United States of America in 1986

Printed in Hong Kong

ISBN 0-312-02192-5

Library of Congress Cataloging-in-Publication Data
Stivers, William.
America's confrontation with revolutionary change
in the Middle East, 1948-1983.
Bibliography: p.
Includes index.
1. Near East—Foreign relations—United States.
2. United States—Foreign relations—Near East.
3. Persian Gulf Region—Foreign relations—United
States.   4. United States—Foreign relations—Persian
Gulf Region.   I. Title.
DS63.2.U5S75   1986   327.73056   85-22318
ISBN 0-312-02192-5

Contents

List of Maps

Preface

This work is a logical – though initially unintended – extension of my earlier book, *Supremacy and Oil*. While focused on US Middle East policy in the post-First World War period, and in particular on the Anglo–American relationship in the region, its underlying theme was much the same as in the present work: when confronted with a vital choice between accommodating nationalist forces in the Middle East, or seeking to repress them, Washington officials constantly chose a policy of repression. From the 1919 Paris Peace Conference all through the 1920s, they made this choice in order to foster a global 'peace' which they equated with the status quo.

The vehicle for securing this peace, in the Washington view, was a comity of 'order-giving' powers – Britain, Italy, France, Japan and the United States – who would join together to keep the world the way it was. Thus, whatever the rhetoric of 'self-determination' and an economic 'open door', American policy makers – Wilsonians as well as their successors – had no intention of giving early independence to the new Arab states carved out of the defeated Ottoman Empire. Rather, the victor powers would assume 'tutelary' authority under the League of Nations Mandate system. Independence might come in the future, but only after the new states had proved they were ready for it, according to the criteria of the advanced powers. It was under this system that France took control of Syria, and Britain of Palestine, Trans-Jordan and Iraq. The United States not only acquiesced in such a division, but actively promoted it, despite numerous entreaties by nationalist leaders, who, both during and after the Paris Peace Conference, promised economic favours in return for American support against Britain and France.

By virtue of the still strong European position – especially the British position – the 1920s constituted a golden age of US policy. In the greater part of the Middle East, the United States could move in the slip-stream of British power, enjoying the economic benefits of an imperial position while avoiding the risks and expenses. By the coming of the Second World War, however, the British Empire was already doomed as a world system; and it would be just a simple matter of time in the postwar period before the United States would have to accept Britain's burdens as 'order-giving power'. During the Eisenhower Administration, the process advanced considerably, although Britain played a special role in US Indian Ocean and Arabian (Persian) Gulf strategy until the end of the 1960s. America's rapid takeover of the British position made its fundamental choices yet more crucial. Would Washington accommodate itself with the forces of radical nationalism in the Middle East, or would it seek to undermine or crush them? As we shall see, the answer to the question was almost identical to the answer given thirty years before.

Of the many individuals and institutions which made this book possible, I wish to note first of all the National Endowment for the Humanities, which provided a research fellowship that made the writing possible. The year of the fellowship was spent in residence at the Carnegie Endowment for International Peace, where I benefited from lavish research support, provided in particular by the reference librarians, Jane Lowenthal and Monica Yin. I thank the President of the Endowment, Thomas Hughes, for offering this invaluable year of residence. I also owe special gratitude to the staff of the Department of the Navy Archives, who were of enormous assistance in helping me gain clearance for work in classified files and in locating these files for my examination. I wish to thank as well Barry Rubin of the Georgetown University Center for Strategic and International Studies for directing me to perspectives on the Kennedy Administration I was not aware of, and Wilma Liebman, who read and vastly improved the chapter on Eisenhower. Finally, portions of the chapter on Eisenhower will appear as an article in a volume edited by Richard Melanson and David Mayers, *Reevaluating Eisenhower: American Foreign Policy in the Fifties*. I thank the publisher, University of Illinois Press, for approval to put this article to dual use.

A note is due here on sources. Many are commonly available. The Declassified Documents Reference System (DDRS) is a magnificently indexed microfilm collection; and the National Security Council documents, are also indexed and on microfilm. The Navy Department documents, as noted, were gained through access to classified files in Navy Department Archives at the Washington Navy Yard. This is an important collection – and generously made available; notes had to be submitted for review, but deletions were negligible. The State Department records concerning early Indian Ocean planning were gained through the hit-and-miss of Freedom of Information Act requests, as were those Defense Department documents not labelled as part of the DDRS collection.

Frankfurt am Main   WILLIAM STIVERS

Note on Interviews

In addition to cited sources, this work is based on interviews with many of the principals, whose contributions I do not reference in notes. I wish, however, to acknowledge my debt to the following individuals: Stuart Barber, former Head of Long-Range Objectives Planning Group, Office of Chief of Naval Operations; Philip Barringer, Attaché, Politico-Military Affairs, US Embassy, London, 1964–6; Admiral Marmaduke Bayne, Chief US Navy representative in 1977–8 Indian Ocean negotiations; Barry Blechman, former Deputy Director, Arms Control and Disarmament Agency; Les Brown, State Department Bureau of Politico-Military Affairs, 1965–78; Admiral Arleigh Burke, Chief of Naval Operations, 1955–61; Leslie Gelb, Head of State Department Bureau of Politico-Military Affairs, 1977–80; Samuel Huntington, National Security Council, 1977–8; Jeffrey Kitchen, Head of State Department Bureau of Politico-Military Affairs, 1961–9; Robert Komer, Under Secretary of Defense for Policy, 1979–81; Haakon Lindjord, US Army, Attaché to State Department Bureau of Politico-Military Affairs during the mid-1960s; George Newman, US Consul General, London, 1964–6; Earl Ravenal, Chief, Asia Division, Office of the Assistant Secretary of Defense for Systems Analysis, 1967–9; Captain Gary Sick, National Security Council; Paul Warnke, Chief Arms Control Negotiator, 1977–9; Admiral Elmo Zumwalt, former Chief of Naval Operations and previously Head of Navy Department Systems Analysis Branch.

Introduction

By New Year 1980 US foreign policy had reached a decisive turn. For the first time in American history Washington policy makers were proclaiming their determination to fight a war for economic reasons alone: America was preparing to go to war for Middle Eastern oil.

The United States had fought other struggles on economic grounds. But never in the past were economic motivations so completely unalloyed, and never had US leaders trumpeted them with such alacrity, as now, at the beginning of the 1980s.

In his State of the Union Address to Congress on 23 January 1980, President Jimmy Carter mapped out the three main factors behind Washington's unprecedented determination: the steady expansion of Soviet military power beyond Soviet borders; an overwhelming Western dependence on oil supplies from the Middle East; and the pressure of social, religious, economic and political change in Third World states, as exemplified by the revolution in Iran.[1] Two thirds of the world's exportable oil, moreover, came from the Persian Gulf and most of it passed through the Strait of Hormuz. Thus, Carter declared, 'An attempt by an outside force to gain control of the Persian Gulf region will be regarded as an assault on the vital interests of the United States of America, and such an assault will be repelled by any means necessary, including military force.'[2]

Carter's sharp words came in response to the Soviet invasion of Afghanistan in December 1979. It would be mistaken, however, to attribute his assertiveness to so immediate a cause. The origins of his policy are not found in the Soviet invasion of Afghanistan, or in the 1973 Arab–Israeli War, or in the heightened awareness in the early 1970s of Western dependence on Persian Gulf oil, or even in the first deployment of Soviet warships to the Indian Ocean in 1968. His readiness to fight for oil had far deeper roots: it stemmed from America's involvement in an interdependent world economy whose prosperity was fuelled by energy resources from the Middle East. Interdependence dictated the need to safeguard the interests of the world economy in order to safeguard American prosperity and strength. Direct US oil dependency on the Middle East, while significant, gave only added force to the already compelling logic of international economic interdependence.

1

AMERICA'S STAKE IN THE WORLD ECONOMY

As a prime factor in US policy, that logic originated in the economic troubles of the 1930s. The Great Depression made its indelible impression on a generation of Washington officials. They learned from that unparalleled economic disaster that in an interdependent world America could not prosper unless the larger world was prosperous. No single country could shield itself from the effects of global deflation, no single economy could maintain full employment and function to the height of its productive potential in the face of contracting world income and trade.

Internationalist leaders of the postwar 'bipartisan consensus' put the lessons they learned into practice. America took the lead in building a new liberal economic order that would encourage trade and growth. At the Bretton Woods Conference, held in July 1944, representatives of the allied governments concluded agreements to set up an International Monetary Fund (to stabilise exchange rates and promote convertibility of currencies) and a World Bank (to help finance economic reconstruction). Both institutions began operations in 1946. On 5 June 1947 Secretary of State George Catlett Marshall, speaking at Harvard, pledged US financial assistance to a comprehensive European recovery programme. From April 1948 until the middle of 1953, over $13.6 billion in US assistance flowed into Western Europe, mainly in the form of products – fuels, fodder, fertilisers, raw materials, machinery and semi-processed goods – that were of critical importance in breaking production bottlenecks.

The US international economic vision was at this point Eurocentric: Washington policy planners began the work of building a more open world economy by rebuilding Europe – along with America, the linchpin of international economic revival. Strategic considerations reinforced the Eurocentric economic focus. Internationalists in both Democratic and Republican parties viewed European and American interests as inseparable. Economic factors and strategic factors were so tightly linked as to be indistinguishable. Security was multifaceted. Productive and fully employed economies, stable social structures, international freedom of trade, enhanced military power – all were parts of the same whole: a secure, liberal world order.

AMERICA'S INTEREST IN EUROPE'S OIL

It was because of America's economic – and security – interdependence with Europe that Washington soon attached supreme importance to Middle Eastern oil. America's own oil needs were met almost entirely from western hemisphere production. But Europe sorely depended on the Persian Gulf. 'The oil of the Middle East', wrote Secretary of State George Marshall in September 1948, 'is an important factor in the success of the European Recovery Program and in the continued prosperity of Europe'.[3]

Indeed, the very success of the recovery programme increased Europe's oil dependency. A National Security Council report of 8 December 1952 discussed why this happened. 'We have', it said,

> encouraged the mechanization of Western Europe. . . . Not only have we given Western Europe large quantities of tanks, combat vehicles, motor transports and aircraft requiring petroleum as fuel, but we have also given its civilians large quantities of machinery and other mechanized equipment. In addition we have urged acceleration of their own production of mechanized equipment. For example production of motor vehicles has increased from a monthly average of 16,400 in 1948 to 150,000 in 1951.

As a result of newly mechanised economies, '[c]urrent demand for petroleum products in Western Europe is about double the demand at the close of World War II'. In fact, European demand was increasing at approximately double the rate in the United States.

The oil to fill the increased demand, the report went on, was 'available only from the Middle East', which contained 'the greatest known petroleum reserves in the world'. 'The postwar mechanization of Europe was predicated on the assumption that Middle Eastern crude oil was, and would continue to be, available to furnish energy for the utilization of the mechanized equipment upon which Europe has become dependent.'[4]

As a leader of the bipartisan, internationalist consensus, Dwight D. Eisenhower agreed completely with the Truman administration's understanding of the importance of Middle Eastern oil. He remarked to his diary on 13 March 1956:

> The oil of the Arab world has grown increasingly important to all of Europe. The economy of Europe would collapse if those oil supplies were cut off. If the economy of Europe would collapse, the United States would be in a situation of which the difficulty could scarcely be exaggerated.[5]

These facts, he stated in a subsequent letter to Winston Churchill, should provide 'a clear guidepost for all our policies, actions, efforts, and propaganda in the region'.[6]

These same facts would lie at the core of US policy up to the present day. The difference between earlier and later periods was that the official concept of international economic interdependence had expanded by the early 1970s. Originally a Eurocentric concept, it now assumed a global character. Europe (and Japan), America's chief allies as well as trading partners, would continue to occupy prime positions in the US constellation of interests, but not so exclusively as during the immediate postwar years: the economic welfare of the *world* as a whole became Washington's vital concern.

THE SOVIET/NATIONALIST THREAT

The postwar economic recovery carried the West to greater heights of prosperity. But this prosperity was not without its perils. Growing energy consumption made Western economies increasingly highly dependent on a pro-Western stability in the Middle East. In the minds of US officials, that stability was endangered by two principal threats. The Soviet Union posed one such threat; and unfriendly indigenous nationalisms posed the second.

Both were disquieting in their own right. The Soviet Union was America's chief military rival in the world; and Soviet control of Middle Eastern oil would weaken Western Europe's ability to resist Soviet demands. Inchoate nationalisms were steeped in anti-Western feeling – resentment over many years of domination by European powers – and even where nationalist leaders were not pro-Soviet, they would seek to dislodge the West from privileged positions in the area.

More disquieting, however, was the interlinking of the Soviet and nationalist threats. For in the eyes of American officials, the Soviets were not likely to gain influence in the Middle East by crude military action or other forms of direct intrusion. Rather, they would take advantage of the 'anti-Western orientation of ultra-nationalist elements' to promote the expulsion from Middle Eastern countries 'of foreigners and foreign-owned property'.[7] They would capitalise, thus, on opportunities they did not create. To stop the Soviets, therefore, the United States would have to eliminate the openings through which the Soviets might enter the situation. This could be done in one of two ways: (1) by co-opting nationalist movements and bringing them into an alignment that, while neutral, tilted West, or (2) by striving to maintain a conservative status quo, opposing nationalist regimes and keeping pro-Western governments everywhere pro-Western.

The choice was an uneasy one. Intellectually, most US administrations understood the power of modern nationalism and felt the need for Washington to accommodate it, if for no other reason than to prevent the Soviet Union from posing as sole benefactor of the nationalist cause. It proved all but impossible, however, to put this understanding into practical effect. For Middle Eastern nationalism presented a great unknown and threatened to upset the established order of things. Policy makers feared that the Soviet Union could exploit this disorder in ways that could not be foretold. Therefore, the United States would have to suppress disorder to keep the Soviets from taking advantage of it. Anti-Sovietism in such a context translated into a general commitment to preserving the status quo against destabilising change. This precluded the strategy of co-option: the choice of four decades of US foreign policy would be to support the status quo and to oppose indigenous forces of movement in the Middle East.

THE STRATEGIC NEXUS

Postwar strategic exigencies added to Washington's anti-nationalist animus. Britain was a power in decline; but in the first postwar decades the British still enjoyed substantial positions of political and military influence in the Middle East. US defence planners wanted to retain this influence. In the words of a 1949 State Department policy paper, it would be 'unrealistic for the United States to undertake its security policy in the Middle East unless the British maintain their strong strategic, political and economic positions in the Middle East and Mediterranean'.[8] In talks with the British during the last three years of the Truman administration, US officials made clear that Washington was planning no 'military sacrifices to retain the countries of the Middle East and Western orbit' and that no American troops would be committed there in the event of global war.[9] The main US role would be to bolster the 'UK primary political and military responsibility in the area with increasing US political, military and economic support'.[10]

The British would occupy a key place in Washington's defence planning for the next twenty years. Until her East of Suez withdrawal (announced in 1968), Great Britain was seen as an integral element of US power in the region. Even as the United States expanded its role it did so not with the aim of diminishing British influence but rather with the aim of concerting actions toward common ends.

The strategic reliance on Britain would clash with the aim of getting closer to nationalists and showing them that America, not the Soviet Union, was the Arabs' true friend. US association with Britain created an identity in Arab eyes between Washington and London. American policy makers knew all too well that this identity between the United States and a detested, colonial power would embarrass American relations with the Arab world – a problem exacerbated by US support of Israel. But despite their knowledge – and despite their acceptance in theory of the need to reach modus vivendi – they could not break the identity because it was based on real identitities of Anglo–American interests and strategy.

Britain's withdrawal from her commitments East of Suez created a military void. Owing to the exigencies of Vietnam, the United States could not fill the void itself. Instead, under the Nixon Doctrine, US strategists looked toward local surrogates – notably the shah's Iran – to safeguard a pro-Western stability in the Persian Gulf. Armed with high quality American weapons, these surrogates would provide the military underpinnings for Western power in the area. America would back them up with an 'over the horizon' naval presence, sustained by a naval and air facility on Diego Garcia, an island outpost in the middle of the Indian Ocean.

Washington policy makers thus embraced military solutions to the problems of the region – not, to be sure, solutions involving a massive, direct US presence, but military nonetheless. They did so at the same time as they realised that such solutions were largely irrelevant to the real issues affecting the peoples of the area, and ultimately, the United States. They had understood this for a long time. The following words from a 1953 National Security Council memorandum could have been written at any time during the postwar era:

> The attainment of US objectives in the area is made difficult by the poverty and the extreme social unrest of populations, the political instability and adminstrative incompetence of existing regimes, the rising tide of nationalism, . . . by United States sponsorship of Israel, and such tensions between countries in the area as the Indian-Pakistan and the Arab-Israel disputes.[11]

Almost twenty years later, a Defense Department official sounded a reprise. He traced the outbreak of violence in the area to unstable local regimes. In the Arabian Peninsula, he remarked, 'many of the governments and societies are highly conservative, and if the leaders fail to make satisfactory progress in political, economic and social reform, conditions could be created that will lead to overthrow of friendly moderate regimes by radicals'.[12]

These assessments – the prevailing official analysis of underlying conditions in the Middle East – suggested glaring defects in the strategy of relying on the military power of local surrogates. First, there was no reason to believe that the complex problems listed above could be resolved through military action. Second, the surrogates were themselves vulnerable to revolutionary change.

So long as the shah maintained surface stability in Iran, Washington did not have to confront the defects in its policy. But when his government spiralled toward ultimate collapse in 1979, the defects became all to clear. Military power could not have saved him from the great underlying forces at work in Iran; and America's remaining 'friends' (in conservative Arab states) suffered from similar internal weaknesses. It made little sense to rely on them to preserve the status quo.

One could also argue that it made little sense to seek military solutions for crises of social upheaval. This was not, however, the conclusion drawn in Washington. Rather, policy makers concluded that the situation now demanded a *greater* application of military power – this time not through surrogates (the shah's demise had shown the shortcomings of that indirect approach) but through a vast increase of US capabilities for unilateral action in the area. And they came to this conclusion despite their recognition, once again, that the instabilities of the region resulted from socio-historical transformations and not from purely military threats: 'ideological rivalries, territorial disputes, the clash between modernizing trends and the forces of tradition, ancient ethnic and religious hatreds, and sheer personal ambition fed by enormous wealth that is at the disposal of some very weak governments'[13] – these, as stated in a 1979 Pentagon study, were overriding sources of tension and conflict in the Persian Gulf.

Thus, when President Carter stated his determination to fight a war for oil, his words marked a culmination of a long process of deepening US involvement in the Persian Gulf. The involvement had deepened because of the structural demands of a foreign policy that placed high value on the American stake in an interdependent, liberal world order. It saw that order imperilled by both the Soviet Union and radical nationalisms that created openings for Soviet expansion. It prescribed increasingly military solutions to problems that were social, political, and economic in origin.

The aim of this book will be to take a closer look at how the United States came to such a pass. It will be a highly critical look, for only at the most fleeting, infrequent junctures did policy makers translate what they knew about reality into programmes that conformed to it. They aligned themselves with a status quo they feared would not last. They sacrificed long-term visions to expedients of the moment. They moved, thus, from one irrelevance to the next, securing, to be sure, a short-run stability, but with no regard for future reckonings.

1 America Moves into the Middle East

The Eisenhower years marked the beginning of direct US activism in the Middle East. In the eyes of US policy makers in the 1950s, the Western oil interest was too vital for Washington to abandon to uncertainty. Nationalist forces were rising in the region – and though not simple handmaidens of the Soviet Union, were steeped in antagonism toward the West. One of the chief causes for this antagonism was the US commitment to Israel – a signal undertaking of the previous Administration. Eisenhower was left the task of trying to reconcile that commitment with the need to still Arab discontent. At the same time, the irreversible decline of British power created a political and military void that only the United States could fill.

To be sure, America's way into the Middle East had been marked out already by President Harry Truman. During Truman's administration, substantial economic and military assistance flowed into Greece and Turkey, and (to a lesser degree) Iran, to form a 'northern tier' palisade against Soviet encroachment on the Suez Canal and Persian Gulf. Yet more significant: it was Truman who committed America to the support of Israel. The United States helped push through the United Nations General Assembly Resolution of 29 November 1947, providing for the partition of Palestine into Arab and Jewish states. On 14 May 1948 – the day the British terminated their Palestine mandate – the new Jewish state was proclaimed in Tel Aviv. Hours later, Truman hastened to recognise it. In January 1949 the Export–Import Bank extended Israel a $100 million credit. In 1950 Israel signed a Point Four agreement with the United States, opening the way further for US economic aid – far exceeding sums given to all the Arab states together.

Yet, in comparison with later years, American involvement was modest. Greece and Turkey lay on the periphery of the Middle East – not at the region's core. Even the key commitment to Israel was by all standards limited. The United States supported Israel politically, and provided considerable economic assistance. Yet Washington supplied no arms and made no commitment to Israel's defence. When, following the proclamation of Israeli statehood, Israel was attacked on all sides by the armies of Egypt, Syria, Lebanon, Jordan and Iraq, the Israelis prevailed, not through US military help, but on the strength of their own superior organisation and resources, coupled with the corruption and incapacity of Arab regimes.

One reason why Washington was not more deeply committed was that it did not have to be. For Western interests in the heart of the region were anchored on a still formidable British presence. In 1952, Great Britain maintained over 64 000 troops in the Middle East – of those, 52 000 (plus 14 000 colonial service troops) were stationed in the gigantic British base along the Suez Canal. British officers seconded to Jordan provided leadership for the Arab Legion. The Royal Air Force operated from 19 airfields in Egypt, Iraq, Jordan, Libya, Cyprus and the Arabian Peninsula; 186 aircraft were stationed at these bases, including 62 combat-ready tactical aircraft at Suez and 3 combat-ready light bombers at Aden. The Royal Navy had bases in Malta, Cyprus, Bahrain, Aden, and in the Suez Canal zone. Three sloops (the equivalent of US Navy destroyer escorts) patrolled the Persian Gulf, supported by three logistics and two survey ships.[1]

British power was impressive. It was, however, progressively weakening – a fact well understood in Washington. In the judgement of a State Department intelligence report 'indigenous social forces are now on the move in the area and, regardless of British actions, will inevitably modify the status quo'. In the short run, British influence was secure in Jordan, Iraq and Libya, in the Persian Gulf emirates and in the Sudan. But now that France was gone from the Levant and Italy from Libya,

> the U.K. has borne the brunt of nationalist attacks. The development of nationalism in the Middle East – and related emergence of a rising middle class dissatisfied with its role in the traditional social and economic structure of the area – has resulted in the gradual discrediting of dynasties, governing groups, personalities, and institutions through which the British exerted their local influence. In addition, Middle East governments and peoples, traditionally impressed by the facts of political and military strength, have noted a steady decline of the U.K. as a world power. As the subordinate U.K. role in the overall U.S.–USSR struggle for power has emerged, the Middle East states are increasingly disposed to challenge the claim of the U.K. to any special position in the region.[2]

The disintegration of Britain's position, already well advanced by 1953, would accelerate during the Eisenhower years. A rising Arab nationalism, combined with sharpened East–West tension in the Middle East, created a perilous situation that the British did not, 'unfortunately, have the ability alone to correct'.[3] Eisenhower would therefore commit Washington to a course of unprecedented direct action in the Middle East.

This action proceeded on four main lines:

1. To strengthen the nothern tier palisade against Soviet expansion, the United States sponsored the Baghdad Pact alliance, comprising Turkey, Iraq, Great Britain, Pakistan and Iran. While the United States never joined the alliance, Washington immediately established military liaison with the Pact organisation. On 1 February 1958 the US formalised this liaison, becoming a full member of a Pact military planning committee.

2. To remove the main cause of Arab animosity against the United States, and in hopes of bringing enduring stability to the area, Washington sought to broker an Arab–Israeli peace.

3. To prevent the West from losing further ground to the Soviets as a result of the ill-starred Anglo–French invasion of Egypt (launched on 31 October 1956 in an effort to sieze control of the Suez Canal) the administration secured congressional passage on 9 March 1957 of the Middle East Resolution, authorising a two-pronged programme providing $200 million a year in economic and military assistance (to be granted to Middle Eastern countries at the president's discretion), plus blanket executive authority 'to use armed forces to assist any nation or a group of such nations requesting assistance against armed aggression from any country controlled by international communism'. Eisenhower had unveiled this programme in his 'Eisenhower Doctrine' address, delivered to the Congress on 5 January 1957.

4. To shore up conservative elements in the region the administration took strong measures to contain the forces of militant nationalism – particularly, orchestrating the 1953 overthrow of Iranian premier Mohammed Mossadegh, an ardent nationalist who had expropriated British oil holdings and undermined the power of the pro-Western shah, and resorting, in 1958, to armed intervention in Lebanon to turn back what seemed to be a pan-Arab threat to the survival of pro-American regimes throughout the area.

In taking such action Eisenhower policy makers were always clear on US stakes in the Middle East. In the words of the president and the secretary of the treasury, Western Europe and the Middle East 'are together the most strategic areas in the world – Western Europe requires Middle Eastern oil and Middle Eastern oil is of importance mainly through its contribution to the Western European economy'.[4]

There was, however, no similar clarity on other issues affecting the US position in the region. American policy makers were plagued by ambivalences. They were torn between the desire to win Arab nationalists over to the West and the practical short-term imperatives of safeguarding Western oil. They wanted to distance the United States from any association with European colonialism at the same time as they relied on British military strength as a key element of Western power in the region. They knew that nationalism and communism were not identical, but feared that Soviet and nationalist objectives – especially the objectives of radical Pan-Arabism – might coincide. They felt that progressive, anti-traditionalist movements were on the ascendancy, yet were unwilling to abandon friendly conservative regimes to uncontrolled change.

Yet, though troublesome, the ambivalences were far from paralysing. When necessity demanded, they were resolved, and resolved decisively, in favour of upholding the status quo.

THE BAGHDAD PACT

During the Truman administration, Anglo–American strategists hatched successive plans for a Middle Eastern Command (MEC)[5] and a Middle Eastern Defence Organisation (MEDO). Both schemes were predicated on strong British leadership, exercised with US backing, and a key role for Egypt. But Arab hostility killed them, leading policy makers to focus on a northern tier defence. On 24 February 1955 the cornerstone was laid for this defence by the signing in Baghdad of a Turko–Iraqi pact. The organisation was joined by Great Britain (5 April), Pakistan (23 September) and Iran (23 October).

Britain was the main Western partner in the Pact, but the United States was involved at the outset in a sponsoring and supporting capacity. Prior to the signing of the Turko–Iraqi treaty on 24 February 1955, American, British and Turkish military planners held talks in London, where they completed a comprehensive study of military objectives, strategy, operational concepts and other matters related to Middle Eastern defence. This study was accepted by the Joint Chiefs of Staff as a point of departure for elaborating an 'allied politico-military concept' for the region. Further Anglo–American conversations took place in Washington over the summer. A US observer sat in on the military planning sessions in Baghdad; and that observer (the US military attaché in Iraq) submitted Pact defence studies for comment to the JCS. This tight liaison was formalised on 1 February 1958, when the United States joined the military planning committee, still without, however, adhering to the treaty.[6]

US objectives were well served by the nothern tier alliance. The United States participated in the development of joint strategic plans and allocated aid according to a collective, regional design. Militarily, the United States bolstered indigenous capacities by providing a nuclear shield (called 'atomic support forces' in the parlance of the times) and helping to improve logistical infrastructure.[7] At the same time the United States spared itself the burdens of *de jure* membership, avoiding intra-Arab disputes and preserving a freer hand in efforts to mediate the Arab–Israeli conflict. The United States did not rule out eventual adherence, but this was made contingent on an Arab–Israeli settlement that would allow Washington to conclude a similar arrangement with Israel.[8]

But the pact also had its costs. It roused intense opposition throughout the Arab world. Egyptian President Nasser denounced the alliance as a transparent device to perpetuate British hegemony. A strong US link to the organisation thus had a political consequence Washington desired to avoid – identification with British imperialism. To realise military advantages, the United States paid a high price in suspicion and mistrust.

Moreover, the pact was short-lived. Its effective use ended on 14 July 1958 when the Hashemite monarchy of Iraq was overthrown in a military coup. The revolutionary leader, General Abd al-Karim Kassem, issued a statement proclaiming a policy of neutralism and nonalignment. US Secretary of State John Foster Dulles tried to step into the breach with a set of bilateral security accords, signed on 31 July 1958, between the United States and Turkey, Pakistan and Iran. These accords, however, did little to retrieve the *de facto* loss of the pact's only Arab member. Iraq formally withdrew from the alliance on 24 March 1959. The remaining members regrouped into the Central Treaty Organisation (CENTO), which continued a moribund existence until the 1979 revolution in Iran.

The United States had every reason to foresee events. Washington officials had accurate intelligence on the internal situation in Iraq. In their view, the ruling elite was a corrupt, feudal oligarchy.[9] The experience could have served as a valuable lesson on the inadvisability of making alliances with narrowly based, unpopular regimes for reasons of short-term military advantage. Such regimes were surrogates of dubious value; and US support for them could only engender bitter feelings toward America. But the lesson, if it was ever learned, was soon forgotten.

AN ARAB–ISRAELI PEACE

Eisenhower and his foreign policy advisers saw a political resolution of the Arab–Israeli conflict as key – perhaps *the* key – to achieving an enduring pro-Western stability in the Middle East. In the view of John Foster Dulles the conflict could 'flare up at any moment'.[10] So long as it remained unsettled, US diplomacy in the area would remain stymied. In the absence of an Arab–Israeli peace, pro-Israel sentiment in Congress precluded US membership in the Baghdad Pact. Arab resentment over loss of territory, plus fears of further Israeli expansion, made it difficult for Washington to convince Arab leaders that the real danger was not Israel, but 'communist imperialism'.[11] Because of its sponsorship of the Jewish state, the US could not compete with the Soviets' anti-Zionist appeal, leaving them with a heavy propaganda advantage. Indeed, in the president's view, Israel was the main impediment to a 'viable' US policy in the area.[12]

Secretary of State Dulles blamed the prior administration for the 'present jam' Washington was in. It had 'always dealt with the area from a political standpoint and had tried to meet the wishes of the Zionists in this country. . . .' The result was a 'basic antagonism with the Arabs' that the 'Russians were now capitalizing on'.[13] Both he and the president were convinced, in the words of a 1953 briefing paper, that 'the U.S. should prove that it has a policy of partial and fair dealing as between the Arab states and Israel'.[14] In his diary entry for 8 March 1956, the president reiterated this belief. '[W]e must be friends with both contestants . . . in order that we can bring them closer together. To take sides could do nothing but to destroy our influence leading toward a peaceful settlement of one of the most explosive situations in the world today.'[15]

Indeed, the administration's desire to project an image of evenhandedness led to the first, and only, instance where the United States achieved its policy aims by imposing sanctions against Israel. In

1953 the Israelis began work on a hydroelectric plant in the Israeli–Syrian demilitarised zone. This project would have diverted Jordan River water to Israel, prompting the Syrian protest that resulted in an order from the chief of the UN Truce Team for Israel to cease work. When the Israelis proceeded with the project the United States stepped in. On 20 October 1953 John Foster Dulles suspended US economic aid to Israel; on 28 October the Israelis abandoned their project, leading to an immediate resumption of US assistance. It proved far more difficult, however, for the United States to broker an Arab–Israeli peace. The two major US efforts to do this failed – illustrating one of the most striking features of Eisenhower's diplomacy: the constant disjuncture between his recognition of fundamental problems that affected US interests in the area and his inability to make any practical advances toward resolving them.

The 1948–9 Arab–Israeli War had left approximately 940 000 Palestinians homeless and destitute. Nearly 70 per cent of the Arab inhabitants of Palestine were displaced during the hostilities. Some fled to escape Israeli violence, others in response to appeals from Arab leaders to evacuate the possible battle zones. Israel refused to readmit them, leaving most to subsist on UN relief. The explosiveness of the situation was confirmed by recurrent waves of reprisals and counter-reprisals along the frontier between Israel and the Gaza Strip, where over 200 000 Palestinian refugees were densely encamped. On 26 August 1955 Secretary Dulles, speaking with the authority of the president, addressed the issue head-on. He proposed a peace settlement linking the guarantee of formally fixed borders with the 'resettlement and, to such an extent that may be feasible, repatriation' of the dispossessed Palestinians, whom Israel would compensate from the proceeds of an international loan subscribed to by the US.[16]

The plan got nowhere. The Arabs wanted substantial territorial concessions whereas Israel was willing to make only minor border rectifications. The Israelis were not willing to consider repatriating the Palestinians. The administration's ability to put any real political weight behind any ideas not meeting Israeli approval was reduced by the fact of impending US elections.

Eisenhower's next peace initiative was shrouded in secrecy. In mid-January he sent former Deputy Secretary of Defense Robert Anderson to the Middle East, empowered to give magnanimous promises of economic aid and Israel in return for an Egyptian–Israeli peace. Anderson shuttled between Cairo and Tel Aviv via Rome or Athens in a small military aircraft. He met on numerous occasions with

Nasser and Israeli Prime Minister David Ben Gurion in an effort that lasted until the middle of March.

The initiative foundered because there were few grounds on which Nasser and Ben Gurion could bridge differences. Ben Gurion refused to accept Anderson as an intermediary and demanded to negotiate with Nasser personally. For domestic political reasons however, it was out of the question for Nasser to conduct face to face negotiations with the Israeli Prime Minister. Ben Gurion had no concessions to offer, to say nothing of what he would have to concede to make a peace treaty palatable to Nasser. Without Israeli willingness to bargain over territory and Palestinian repatriation, no amounts of American largesse would induce Nasser to conclude an Egyptian–Israeli peace.[17]

THE EISENHOWER DOCTRINE

The Anderson Mission marked the last administration initiative to sponsor an overall settlement to the Arab–Israeli conflict. The lack of any further initiative is surprising in view of the continued belief, as articulated in a 1960 NSC memorandum on US Middle Eastern policy, that 'any advance toward solution of the Arab–Israel dispute, particularly the refugee problem, would be very much in the interest of the United States'.[18] It is not surprising, however, in view of Washington's post-Suez stress on resisting 'communism' – and its concomitant playing down of concern with the Arab–Israeli conflict.

In the president's 'Eisenhower Doctrine' address of 5 January 1957 – the basis of the Middle East Resolution enacted on 9 March – he noted that his programme would not touch the 'problems of Palestine and relations between Israel and the Arab states and the future of the Arab refugees'. The UN was dealing with these problems and the United States was supporting the UN. The United States would put primary emphasis on aid to friendly states, including direct military intervention, if necessary, 'to secure and protect the territorial integrity and political independence of such nations, requesting such aid, against overt armed aggression from any nation controlled by International Communism'.[19]

The terms of the President's message seemed clear. He was calling for resistance to Soviet 'aggression'. Yet it contained phrasings that allowed for a significant expansion of rationales. He had not bothered to explain what it meant to be 'controlled by International Communism' as opposed simply to being communist. He also adverted to the possibility of 'indirect' communist aggression – a term of little specificity. The Middle East Resolution itself referred to international communism's efforts to dominate 'free and independent people' through the use of 'economic pressure' and 'internal subversion'.[20]

In practice, the administration never employed its authority under the Middle East Resolution against Soviet 'aggression'. The first use of it was an emergency $10 million economic assistance grant to Jordan, effected on 29 April 1957, followed (on 29 June) by a second $10 million infusion of economic aid, plus a military assistance grant of the same sum. Between 25 April and 3 May, the Sixth Fleet was present in Eastern Mediterranean waters to display Washington's support for King Hussein.[21] Throughout the crisis – lasting roughly from February to the beginning of May – policy makers knew that the threat to the King's throne stemmed from 'internal forces' inspired not by Moscow but by Cairo and Pan-Arabism.[22] As we shall see, much the same features characterised anti-government forces in Lebanon, where US Marines landed in July 1958, in the midst of a civil war. Thus, despite the anti-Sovietism of US rhetoric, the chief use of the Middle East Resolution came in defence of conservative elites against pan-Arabism and internal change.

PAN-ARABISM AND THE USSR

Yet, in the view of Eisenhower policy makers, American intervention in internal struggles contradicted only the letter of the Middle East Resolution. For in the real world it was not possible to make fine distinctions betwen revolutionary nationalism on the one side, and Soviet expansionism on the other: there were many instances where they might be mutually supportive, and in a way detrimental to Western interests. However, US officials were also aware that indiscriminate opposition to nationalism, joined with American ties to Europe and Israel, could give the Soviet Union just the opportunity it wanted to make political inroads in Afro–Asian states. NSC 5820/1, a comprehensive review of US Middle Eastern policy, approved by the president on 4 November 1958, illustrates the ambivalences arising from these conflicting perceptions.

The document painted a grim picture. Political trends in the Middle East, it said, 'are inimical to U.S. and other Western interests'. Since 1956, 'the West and the radical pan-Arab nationalist movement have been arrayed against each other', as the West supported conservative regimes opposed to radical nationalism. In 1958, the conservative resistance collapsed, 'leaving the radical nationalist regimes almost without opposition in the area'.

The most dangerous challenge, however, arose 'not from Arab nationalism *per se*, but from the coincidence of many of its objectives with many of those of the USSR and the resultant way in which it can be manipulated to serve Soviet ends'. These ends consisted of the weakening and ultimate elimination of Western influence, 'using Arab nationalism as an instrument, and substituting Soviet influence for that of the West'. Washington's ability to keep the Russians from achieving their goals depended upon how closely the United States could work 'with Arab nationalism and associate itself . . . with such aims and aspirations of the Arab people as are not contrary to the basic interests of the United States'.

But the United States could not go too far in getting closer to nationalist regimes: 'We face the fact that certain aspects of the drive toward Arab unity, particularly as led by Nasser, are strongly inimical to our interests.' Any US approaches toward Nasser, therefore, had to be undertaken in such a way as to maintain freedom of action in dealing with other Arab leaders, who would be given discreet encouragement whenever 'we see signs of independent [anti-Nasser] views . . .'.

Thus, the United States would 'endeavor to establish an effective working relationship with Arab nationalism while at the same time seeking constructively to influence and stabilize the movement and to contain its outward thrust'. When the 'essentially neutralist character of pan-Arab nationalism' precluded 'maintenance of the special political, military and economic interests comprising the Western position in the area', the United States would be prepared 'if necessary' to make 'appropriate revisions in the existing Western strategic position'. But Washington would try to keep such revisions at a minimum, retaining as much of the special Western interests as it could. Moreover, all such policy guidelines subserved the two 'primary objectives' it was 'essential' that Washington achieve: 1) 'Denial of the area to Soviet domination', and 2) 'Continued availability of sufficient Near Eastern oil to meet vital Western European requirements on reasonable terms'.[23]

To a point, there was considerable wisdom in this curious *pot pourri*. Eisenhower policy makers knew that it would be counterproductive to launch a frontal attack on pan-Arab nationalism: hence, their advocacy of ostensible accomodation conjoined with discreet encouragement of 'independent' leaders. But the idea that the United States could move closer to something called 'Arab nationalism *per se*', distinct from a nationalism whose objectives coincided with the Soviet Union's, was an exercise in delusion, for it is hard to conceive of an Arab nationalism that did not share the Soviet objective of diminished Western influence. It is also hard to conceive of how the administration could reconcile its fundamental Eurocentricism with a policy of accommodating nationalist demands.

The Eisenhower advisers hoped to square the circle through tactical finesse – getting closer to Arab nationalists, but not too close; giving up some privileged positions, but only to the minimum extent required; supporting pro-Western, anti-Nasser regimes, but not so obviously as to let the Soviets pose as sole champion of Arab unity. Yet no amount of finesse could spare US policy makers the ultimate burden of hard choice; and when hard choices were made, they invariably followed the logic maintaining conservative, pro-Western 'stability' in the region.

DEFENDING THE CONSERVATIVE STATUS QUO

Eisenhower encountered his first test before his inauguration. Following the nationalisation of the Anglo–Iranian Oil Company (AIOC) holdings on 30 April 1951, the British company (in which the government owned a majority share) was joined by the other six major world oil companies in a devastating boycott of Iranian oil. Denied access to world oil markets, Iran suffered progressive economic deterioration and resultant political disorder. In an appeal sent to the president-elect on 9 January 1953, Prime Minister Mossadegh expressed the hope that Eisenhower, as president, would give 'careful consideration' to the Iranian case.

Eisenhower's response, dated 10 January, offered assurances that he would study Mossadegh's views 'with care and sympathetic concern'. At the end of May, Mossadegh sent a second dispatch, asking Eisenhower either to help in removing the obstacles to Iranian oil sales or to give economic assistance enabling Iran to use other resources. This time (waiting over a month before sending his reply) Eisenhower responded with an explicit refusal.[24]

Leaked by Mossadegh's political enemies, the news of Eisenhower's refusal further weakened the prime minister's tenuous grip on power.[25]

This was in fact what the Administration desired: for on 22 July, approval had been given to a CIA scheme to stage a coup against Mossadegh. CIA operative Kermit Roosevelt went to Iran in mid-July. He made contact with the shah, with retired General Fazlollah Zahedi (whom the shah would appoint prime minister in place of Mossadegh), and with dissident army and police officers. On 18 August, a CIA-financed mob and anti-Mossadegh army elements took to the streets, terrorising the prime minister's supporters. Zahedi took power the next day. US aid followed quickly – first, $900 000 directly out of a CIA safe, and then a $45 million emergency grant, announced on 5 September. In October 1954 the Iranian parliament ratified an oil settlement: in place of the AIOC monopoly, an international consortium would purchase and distribute Iranian production; 40 per cent of the shares in this new enterprise would be held equally by five large American oil firms.[26] The first CIA-sponsored overthrow of a foreign government seemed a thoroughgoing success.

Eisenhower's aversion to dealing with Mossadegh was rooted in the President's uneasy assessment of the relationship between militant nationalism and 'international communism'. In Eisenhower's view, Mossadegh had caused political and economic disruption in Iran by refusing to settle the oil dispute with Britain. Faced with deepening political crisis, Mossadegh, though noncommunist, accepted the communists' support, thinking he could outwit them. But, the president thought, 'Dr. Mossadegh would become to Iran what the ill-fated Dr. Benes had been in Czechoslovakia – a leader whom the Communists, having gained power, would eventually destroy'.[27] Thus, in order to halt Iran's slide into communism, it was necessary to overthrow the country's nationalist premier (who had invited American support).

In testimony before the Senate Foreign Relations Committee on 29 April 1953, John Foster Dulles put this sort of reasoning in a global context. The area all the way from Turkey to Japan and Korea was 'soft', the Secretary declared. It was filled with 'social problems and unrest which would exist if there were no such thing as Soviet communism in the world'. In a peaceful world, where the Soviet Union posed no threat, America could do much to promote reform and self government. But since the Soviets were adroit at capturing 'the so-called reform and revolutionary movement', the United States had no realistic alternative but to support status quo regimes. Under normal circumstances, Dulles said, '[w]e would be trying to get somebody else, but in times like these, in the unrest of the world today, and the divided spirit, we know that we cannot make a transition without losing control of the whole situation'.[28]

These thoughts stand in sharp contrast with the vision of an ascendant nationalism that both Eisenhower and Dulles wanted to win over to the West. But to act on that vision would run the risk of 'losing control'. It was this same fear of losing control that led Eisenhower, in 1958, again to identify US interests with the conservative status quo, and to order a Marine intervention in the civil war in Lebanon.

The civil war erupted in May 1958. The immediate, precipitating cause was the well-founded rumour that the pro-American, Maronite Catholic President, Camille Chamoun, was angling to change the Lebanese constitution, which limited him to one term in office, in order to secure re-election. The more fundamental cause had to do with unequal Moslem access to political power.

In his memoirs Eisenhower asserts, '[b]ehind everything was our deep-seated conviction that the Communists were principally responsible for the "trouble" in Lebanon'.[29] It is doubtful that Eisenhower really thought this at the time. As Robert Murphy, then undersecretary of state for political affairs, later recorded, 'Much of the conflict concerned personalities and rivalries of a domestic nature. . . . Communism was playing no direct or substantial part in the insurrection, although Communists no doubt hoped to profit from the disorders. . . . The outside influences came mostly from Egypt and Syria.'[30] In a White House meeting held on 15 June, CIA Director Allen Dulles said much the same: the Soviets, he stated (with Eisenhower present), 'have not entered the Lebanese situation at all except by radio'.[31]

Eisenhower's determination to safeguard the status quo in Lebanon, despite the lack of an appreciable Communist role in the rebellion, was reinforced by the conjuncture of events. President Chamoun had established firm pro-Western credentials by embracing the Eisenhower Doctrine. He had, in consequence, exposed himself to intensified political attack by advocates of Arab unity. In Syria, pan-Arab tendencies had steadily gathered strength, culminating in the United Arab Republic (UAR), a union between Egypt and Syria proclaimed on 1 February 1958. In such a context it was extremely important to back Chamoun. For if a pro-Western leader like Chamoun called for help and the United States did not respond, as Dulles warned on 15 June, 'that will be the end of every pro-Western government in the area'. Eisenhower agreed, noting that 'in such circumstances we would have to fulfill our commitments'. [32]

Notwithstanding their desire to end the rebellion, policy makers approached the idea of a Lebanon intervention with ample misgivings. Chamoun's first appeal for help came at the outset of the rebellion in May; US Marines were not ordered to Lebanon until mid-July. Eisenhower understood the pitfalls of intervention: rather than solving Lebanon's problems, an intervention by Western forces might inflame confessional strife and lead to territorial partition. Arab resentment over such an action could overwhelm pro-Western leaders in other countries. Therefore, Washington officials were hopeful that they could avoid intervention.[33]

These hopes were dashed, however, on 14 July 1958, when the Hashemite monarchy of Iraq was overthrown in a military coup. In Washington's estimate the revolutionaries were clearly Nasser sympathisers. There was now no doubt in Eisenhower's mind that the United States – Chamoun had made a frantic request for help to the US Ambassador in Beirut – would have to intervene in Lebanon. Given the upheaval in Iraq, the United States had no choice: failure to respond to Chamoun's appeal would 'set up a chain reaction which will doom the pro-West governments of Lebanon and Jordan and Saudi Arabia and raise grave problems for Turkey and Iran'.[34] The time had come, Eisenhower believed, 'to stop the trend toward chaos'.[35]

When Eisenhower announced the Marine landings on 15 July, he invoked the Communist threat.[36] In private, however, there was no need to blur the fact that pan-Arab radicalism was the immediate concern. Meeting with the president on 23 July, Secretary Dulles likened Arab nationalism to a 'flood which is running strongly'. 'We cannot,' he said, 'successfully oppose it, but we can put up sandbags around positions we must protect – the first group being Israel and Lebanon and the second being the oil positions around the Persian Gulf.' The president proceeded to expand on the secretary's assessment. Ultimately, the Western positions could not be held 'against the underlying and often unthinking convictions of the Arab world'. The United States, he said, had to find some way to change those convictions, in order to 'get ourselves to the point where the Arabs will not be hostile to us'.[37] He offered no ideas on how to do this.

THE SUEZ CONUNDRUM

In view of the antinationalist sentiment – really a fear of change – that motivated his actions in Iran and Lebanon, Eisenhower's behaviour during the Suez crisis presents a stark anomaly. For instead of siding with Israel, Britain and France to strike Nasser down, he opposed their use of force and pressured them to withdraw from Egyptian territory they had captured in Sinai and at the mouth of the canal. He succeeded through a tough diplomacy: denying emergency oil shipments to Britain and France (Nasser had blocked all traffic through the Canal in response to the allies' attack), using US power in the International Monetary Fund to refuse Britain access to IMF resources needed to stem a run on the pound, and threatening Israel with US participation in UN economic sanctions.

The anomaly, however, was only apparent. Eisenhower did not disagree with the allies on fundamental interests: rather, as we shall see, his disagreements were almost purely *tactical*.

On 26 July 1956 Egyptian President Gamal Abdul Nasser nationalised the Anglo–French-owned Suez Canal Company. Nasser's nationalisation decree came one week after the United States reneged on an earlier offer to help finance the Aswan Dam – a giant hydroelectric and irrigation project on the upper Nile to which Nasser had accorded the highest priority. Egypt, Nasser said in a public address announcing the Canal expropriation, would apply profits from the tolls toward building the Dam.

From the outset, the Anglo–French impulse was to reverse Nasser's move through force. Britain and France began as early as 28 July to lay plans and muster forces for an attack on Egypt. The attack was delayed at first on account of simple unpreparedness, and then because of London's desire to find a suitable pretext on which to act. Finally, on 22 and 23 October, Israel, Britain and France agreed on a battle plan. Israeli forces would drive into the Sinai peninsula. Acting under the pretext of protecting the Canal, Britain and France would issue an ultimatum demanding that within twelve hours both Egypt and Israel distance their forces at least ten miles from the waterway. When Egypt inevitably refused – an Egypt withdrawal would have conceded Israeli occupation of nearly the whole of the Sinai – the British and French would seize the Canal, purportedly to insure free passage.

The Israeli attack came on 19 October. The Anglo–French ultimatum followed the next day; and on 31 October British and French warplanes started bombing Egyptian bases. An Anglo–French paratroop drop on 5 November preceded a naval bombardment and amphibious assault on the 6th.

Eisenhower opposed the use of force. It was an opposition, however, that stemmed almost entirely from tactical considerations.

Eisenhower did not like the nationalisation: roughly 75 per cent of Eurpoe's oil came from the Middle East, and of that, two thirds went through the Canal. Thus, in the president's view, Nasser's control of the Canal put Europe in economic peril.[38] But he conceded that 'world public opinion was largely on [Nasser's] side'. Indiscriminate military action, without proper justification, would be counter-productive. Afro–Asian countries would unite against the West, providing an opening for sure Soviet gains. There might, of course, be instances that called for military action. But Suez was 'the wrong issue about which to be tough'.[39]

None of this implied an affinity for Nasser. Even after the attack, Eisenhower stated that 'he did not fancy helping Egypt'. But he had to nonetheless. The United States had been signatory (along with Britain and France) to the Tripartite Declaration of 25 May 1950. It had pledged in the declaration to take immediate action to stop any violation of frontiers or armistice lines. If the United States did not fulfill its pledge, US prestige would decline in Arab eyes and the Soviets would enter the picture.[40] He could not afford, moreover, to stand behind Israel, Britain and France against the opinion of most of the world.

Yet he still shared his allies' view of the Egyptian leader. He regarded him as an 'evil influence'. His complaint with the British and French was that 'they chose a bad time and incident on which to launch corrective measures'. Preferring a flanking action to a frontal assault, he stressed the advisability of building up an Arab rival to Nasser (King Saud was his candidate): 'if we could build him up as the individual who captured the imagination of the Arab world, Nasser would not last long.'[41]

Eisenhower had come to a hostile view of Nasser months before Egypt nationalised the Suez Canal. When Nasser assumed the premiership of Egypt in April 1954, Washington hoped to win him to a pro-Western alignment. CIA agents Kermit Roosevelt and Miles Copeland became good friends with Nasser, meeting with him on almost a daily basis. But US hopes of winning Nasser over were soon dashed.

On 28 April 1955 Israel launched a fierce reprisal raid into the Gaza Strip, revealing Egypt's military impotence. Nasser began looking for arms. When Western countries turned him down, he looked to the Soviet bloc. In July he concluded an arms agreement with Czecho-slovakia, which he announced on 27 September 1955, much to Washington's dismay.

Nasser had already started to slip from US favour with his opposition to the Baghdad Pact and his espousal of neutralism at the Bandung Conference of Afro–Asian leaders in April 1955. But rather than confront him, the administration tried now to purchase friendship. Spurred by the Czech arms deal, the US offered in December 1955 to grant $56 million for the first stage of Aswan Dam construction. The American offer was accompanied by commitments for a $14 million grant and $200 million loan, from Britain and the World Bank respectively.

But the aid had strings; in particular, Egypt would have to submit herself to an anti-inflationary domestic policy supervised by the World Bank. Resentful over such conditions, Nasser stalled for better terms. In the meantime the Egyptian press waged a bitter propaganda campaign against the Baghdad Pact, the West's refusal to sell Egypt arms, and Western support for Israel. Rumours circulated that Nasser was talking with the Soviets about financing the dam.

Eisenhower was coming to the position that Nasser was largely responsible for the ills of the region. The failure of the Anderson Mission etched this impression indelibly in Eisenhower's mind. The mission failed because of the mutual incompatability of the Israeli and Egyptian positions. But when the failure had become patent in early March 1956, Eisenhower put almost the entire burden of blame on Nasser. 'We have reached the point', he noted in his diary entry for 8 March, 'where it looks as if Egypt under Nasser is going to make no move whatsoever to meet the Israelites in an effort to settle outstanding differences'. On account of Soviet arms, the Arabs were becoming more arrogant by the day, 'and disregarding the interests of Western Europe and the United States in the Middle East'.[42]

His response was to approve a programme, drawn up by Dulles on 28 March, to punish and isolate Egypt. The programme comprised: continued denial of arms export licenses, delay in concluding the Aswan Dam negotiations, delay in granting oil and grain to Egypt under the PL 480 program, holding in abeyance decisions on the CARE program for Egypt, increased aid to pro-Western regimes and political forces in Libya, Ethiopia, Lebanon and Saudi Arabia, and stepped-up support to the Baghdad Pact. These measures, as Dulles put it, would 'let Colonel Nasser realise that he cannot cooperate as he is doing with the Soviet Union and at the same time enjoy most-favored nation treatment from the United States'.[43] The subsequent US withdrawal from the Aswan project – announced to Egypt in a meeting on 19 July between Dulles and Egyptian Ambassador Ahmed

Hussein – was consistent with the anti-Nasser offensive that Eisenhower envisioned in March. Thus, as of early 1956, Washington and Cairo were antagonists. Eisenhower had failed the most critical test of his ability to achieve a modus vivendi with Arab nationalism.

EISENHOWER'S EFFECT ON FUTURE US POLICY

None of Eisenhower's failures was costly in the short run. Indeed, in the short run, Eisenhower achieved what he desired. Pro-Western regimes in the area remained pro-Western and European oil supplies remained secure.

These successes, however, were not all Eisenhower's doing. He was helped by the fact that 'radical' forces in the Middle East were divided and often at odds with each other. In the last two years of the Eisenhower presidency, the pan-Arab movement lost steam. Iraq's Premier Kassem rejected union with Egypt and Syria. Nasser's support of Kassem's pro-union opposition incited a virulent Egyptian–Iraqi propaganda struggle. In the meantime disaffection mounted in Syria over Egyptian domination of the UAR; Syria would withdraw from it in September 1961 after an army-led revolt. Finally, administration fears of adroit Soviet exploitation of opportunities in the region were overwrought. Rather than turning the turbulent politics of the area to their advantage, the Soviets found themselves in a house of mirrors, aiding two regimes which hated each other (Egypt and Iraq), and in a quandary over whether to aid local communists at the risk of alienating the noncommunist nationalist leaders who held power. Soviet bloc arms shipments to Egypt, and eventual Soviet financing of the Aswan Dam, did not dissuade Nasser from a harsh repression of Egyptian (and later Syrian) communists.

Judged from a long-run perspective, Eisenhower's apparent successes quickly pale. The United States enjoyed unprecedented leverage in the Middle East; it would probably never enjoy such leverage again. This leverage was not put to full constructive use. The administration addressed no concerted effort toward resolving the Palestinian problem; and after 1956, no attempt was made to broker an Arab–Israeli peace. Eisenhower thus bequeathed to his successors a virulent conflict that would go, at best, into sporadic remission before the next explosive outbreak. His ability to bring about a settlement was greater than any president who followed; hence, his failure to act when he had the chance imposed heavy burdens on future US leaders.

The president's failings, moreover, came not solely through default. In the case of Iran he did direct damage to the interests he thought he was defending. The overthrow of Mossadegh delegitimised the shah's regime, and ultimately brought on a revolution bred in anti-Americanism. Eisenhower thus threw away an opportunity to help consolidate a noncommunist nationalism that, if allowed to develop, would have provided a far more solid bulwark of stability in the region than a personalised monarchy that never outlived the discredit of having been installed by Washington.

Yet, even as we note (in hindsight) the failures of Eisenhower's policies, we cannot draw the ready conclusion that another president, surrounded by different advisors, would have behaved differently. For, as we shall see in the remaining chapters, succeeding administrations acted on the same premises, pursued the same basic goals, and made nearly the same mistakes as Eisenhower did in the 1950s. Faces changed, and so did tactics – but underlying objectives and rationales survived, untouched by time.

2 The Strategic Formulation

Decolonisation would transform the strategic topography of the world. Newly independent states could turn not only against the West, but also against each other, sparking local conflicts that could expand in wider, and more dangerous, directions. At the same time, the loss of territory to Western control would make it all the more difficult to maintain the military presence which seemed so urgent in view of portentous shifts in global power. Nowhere would such currents of change be so powerful as on the littoral of the Indian Ocean.

This is how forward-thinking military planners viewed the world by the end of the 1950s. The Indian Ocean was to them an area of supreme importance – a strategic region where the stresses of nation-building and modernisation would engender chronic instabilities threatening to the West.

Implicitly, they disputed Eisenhower's strategy for the Middle East. Eisenhower, despite various shifts and nuances of policy, sought to safeguard Western interests by calming the Arab–Israeli conflict, by stemming the tide of pan-Arabism, and by containing the Soviet Union behind a northern-tier palisade. For an important group of military strategists, however, the president was missing the vital point that the ultimate Western interest was in the Persian Gulf itself – and to protect that interest the United States might need to enter the area with armed force. Moreover, in their view, the Indian Ocean and Persian Gulf were geopolitically linked: to avail themselves of military power in the Persian Gulf, Western states would have to use the Indian Ocean as the prime base of operations and avenue of approach.

The Department of the Navy was the prime natural locus of early US strategic thinking about the Indian Ocean region. Naval planners were among the first to define both the challenge and the response. It is a testament to their acuity that so much of their analysis stood the test of time. It is likewise a testament to bureaucratic steadfastness that so much of their strategic prescriptions have carried over to the present day. For current policies (not to mention underlying world views) can be traced on a straight line to navalist thinking stretching through the 1960s back to Eisenhower's second term. It is here that we discover essential formulations and concepts of interest which help explain US actions of the moment.

28

The Indian Ocean

Source: US, Department of the Army, Defense Mapping Agency Topographic Center, *South Asia, A Bibliographic Survey* (Washington, DC: Government Printing Office, 1973), printed in Monoranjan Bezboruah, *U.S. Strategy in the Indian Ocean* (London and New York: Praeger Publishers, 1977).

DECOLONISATION: THE STRATEGIC VIEW

Unlike some civilian officials, naval planners were not torn between the desire to curry favour with indigenous nationalisms on the one hand, and strategic imperatives on the other. Since the strategic equation was their chief concern, they mourned the death of imperial systems whose passing posed fresh problems for the United States. In a memorandum dated 5 September 1958, Admiral Roy L. Johnson, Director of the Navy Department's Long-Range Objectives Planning Group, highlighted one factor behind the Navy's misgivings: 'as dismemberment of friendly colonial empires into neutralist nationalisms proceeds', he wrote, the United States would lose access to foreign bases and ports vital for sustained naval operations.[1]

The contrast between 'friendly colonial empires' and uncooperative 'neutralist nationalisms' speaks for itself in reflecting a fundamental view of the world. Such a contrast would be insignificant if it reflected the attitude of a sole individual. But it did not. Throughout the Navy Department, strategists saw decolonisation mainly as a threat to Western power.

The nature of this threat was drawn out in a sweeping stroke by a 1960 Navy Department memorandum prepared as part of a wider National Security Council study of impending global power shifts over the next five to ten years. According to the Navy's analysts, virtually all of Africa would obtain independence or autonomy 'often associated with an increased drift from Western influence'. The same would happen in the Middle and Far East. As a result of this trend, Western air, land and naval forces would be expelled from their bases and staging posts. Moreover, there could be no guarantee of aircraft landing or overflight privileges. Neither could naval commanders count on secure port facilities to fuel, repair or provision their vessels. All could be denied whenever a local government saw fit – and it was during times of crisis, when forces were needed most, that such denial would most likely occur.

Standing in the wings, eager to capitalise on Western decline, was the Soviet Union. In the view of US strategists, it would be just a matter of time before the Soviets 'exhibited' their interest in the Indian Ocean with a naval presence. But Soviet military capabilities were not seen as the major problem. The Soviets would never be able to replicate the imperial experience of the West. Their options were much more limited, but still disturbing. For the very fact of Western imperialism left a legacy of bitterness in the Thirld World. Thus, the economic weakness and political instability of emerging states could offer opportunities for Soviet penetration, 'particularly when accompanied by anti-Western attitudes, as in much of the former or remaining colonial areas'. Under the 'guise of peace and anti-imperialism' the Soviets might make common cause with anti-Western elements to press for UN action to restrict support of Western military capabilities by member nations.[2] The effect of this concerted agitation would be to render mainland facilities unsafe – particularly so when the increase in new African states 'gives the under-developed nations a majority vote' in the UN. And 'friendly colonial empires' which had provided comfort in the past would prove increasingly useless in the years ahead. First, by the end of the 1960s there would not be many of them left. But even the territories which remained under European control – such as Portuguese Mozambique – would prove of scant use, for in the new age of Afro–Asian nationalism, the United States could only inflame Third World animosity if it based its military position on collaboration with detested colonial powers. Thus, rather than rely on its European friends, Washington would have to keep distance from them.[3]

And America would have no greater luck exploiting the sympathies of pro-Western elites in the Third World. In many areas, indigenous resources for resistance would be inadequate following European withdrawal. Coups, insurgencies and fragile economies would all contribute to endemic instability. When combined with external pressures – whether exerted directly by the Soviet Union or by 'Communist-oriented' nationalist regimes – large areas of the Indian Ocean littoral might succumb to neutralisation 'by contagion or intimidation, with resultant weakening of their ultimate resistance to Communist pressures'.[4]

Thus, for US naval strategists, decolonisation would upset the balance of power in Africa and the Persian Gulf. They had no doubts as to what was needed to set the balance right: the United States would have to sustain a military presence in the Indian Ocean, both to support US prestige with displays of force, and, when required, to 'intervene promptly to defeat aggression or subversion, restore order, and/or evacuate Western inhabitants'.[5]

While these interventions might in some cases be aimed at defeating or deterring Soviet bloc interference, it is quite clear that policy makers were more concerned with controlling the *internal* developments of African and Persian Gulf states, supporting 'friendly governments',[6] and forestalling 'local Communist coups'.[7] For inasmuch as the Soviet Union threatened Western interests in the region, it did so in proportion to opportunities – afforded by circumstance – for political, economic and military penetration. Cutting off Soviet advances did not imply a high probability of confrontation with Soviet forces. It meant rather that through timely interventions ashore, the United States could eliminate opportunities the Soviets might chance to exploit. Anti-Sovietism in this context translated into a general opposition to internal dissidence (often associated with local 'Communism') and destabilising 'radical' nationalisms.

SEA POWER IN THE POST-COLONIAL WORLD

In the navalist view, sea power would afford the most effective means of assuring pro-Western stability in the region of impending crisis. The absence of continental bases and garrisons would place a premium on sea-going striking power – on amphibious assault capabilities, on the capacity to deploy forces rapidly from one trouble spot to another without having to ask permission to do so. Serving as floating depots and staging posts, naval vessels could fulfill such needs independent of 'foreign bases, use of which may be subject to denial or delay'.[8]

To be sure, there were ample disagreements over the scope and the nature of US Indian Ocean deployments. Some officials felt that modest 'show of force' operations would be sufficient, to be augmented by attack carriers when need arose.[9] Ships thus assigned to Indian Ocean duty would be detached from the Pacific or Mediterranean. Others, however, saw need for a separate Indian Ocean fleet.

Admiral Arleigh Burke, Chief of Naval Operations from 1955 to 1961, advocated the second course. His interest in an Indian Ocean fleet dated from the late 1940s, when he had already written the British off. Owing to the bureaucratic climate of the times, he could do little more than try to get his colleagues to start thinking about the future US role in the Indian Ocean. By 1961, the time was ripe to bring the question into the open. The new Kennedy administration was alive to the prospects of limited war in the Third World. Thus, when Burke discussed Indian Ocean requirements with Secretary of the Navy John B. Connally in early 1961, he was speaking to a receptive party. The question was submitted for re-examination, with Burke instructing a Navy study group to 'get a lot of general naval philosophy' into their work.[10]

Aside from any strategic rationale, the Navy had strong bureaucratic reasons for entering the Indian Ocean. The Eisenhower administration had sought to contain defence spending by undercutting US conventional capacities in favour of reliance on nuclear deterrence. While the Navy acquiesced in this policy, it did not embrace it with relish. In June 1954 the Navy's Strategic Plans Division warned that planned increases in strategic retaliatory power would cause reductions in amphibious warfare vessels and auxiliary ships – both essential for rapid Navy and Marine Corps mobility in limited war situations. In May, it had raised fundamental questions about administration strategy: how prudent was it to leave the United States with no choice but to accept 'local aggression' or unleash nuclear war?[11]

During the Eisenhower years, the aircraft carrier had been spared the axe because it could perform a nuclear retaliatory role. By the end of the 1950s, naval planners estimated that missile launching submarines would take over the carrier's strategic role by 1965. This meant that the carrier fleet would soon be stripped of a prime mission. But the Navy was never enthusiastic about having to use its prized capital ship for nuclear retaliation. The Polaris submarine would relieve the carrier of an unwanted responsibility that the Navy would replace with another which was more desirable – limited war. In the words of the 1958 Long-Range Objectives Plan:

> The primary mission of carrier strike forces during the period 1963–73 will be to provide a prompt, versatile, and effective component of national capability for inhibiting or coping with limited wars. The aircraft carrier will provide a mobile air base to satisfy requirements in areas where pre-stocked, politically unencumbered air bases are not available or are insufficient.[12]

The Indian Ocean was rimmed by potential crisis areas which met the conditions described above. It was scarcely accidental that talk of Indian Ocean deployments coincided with the Navy's need to propound a limited war rationale for the carrier. There was, moreover, the question of numbers. The Navy claimed a need for eighteen carriers but knew that fifteen was the best it could expect, accounting for fiscal realities.[13] But whatever the number, carrier advocates could strengthen their case by finding a new ocean in which to operate. Thus, bureaucratic interests combined with the reality of world upheaval to reinforce naval prescriptions for dealing with disorder and revolution in the Indian Ocean littoral.

STRATEGIC ISLANDS

As plans for Indian Ocean deployments ripened, so did plans for bases to support them. Freedom from mainland facilities constituted one of the key arguments for placing primary reliance on sea power as Washington's military trump in the region. However, naval forces themselves needed base support. The Indian Ocean was a huge area. If resupply came solely by sea, the effectiveness of US forces would be compromised. Without secure refuelling facilities, for example, a task force might have to reduce speed simply to preserve oil. Likewise, repair and communications would be more difficult; and the prolonged stationing of a task force would wear more quickly on equipment and men.

The Navy began to consider, then, the issue of bases. Some officers, keen on the idea of getting something for free, proposed in 1960 to take over facilities in Kenya – at Mombasa. This was rejected on the grounds that it would prove 'a very short-term mainland base'.[14] Beforehand, in 1959, members of the Long-Range Objectives Group had mulled over the problem and devised a solution more in keeping with political realities: instead of basing US power on the whims of what one official called 'bitchy little nations who wouldn't let us in', the Navy would have to resort to 'strategic islands' – sparsely populated territories, immune from pressures for independence, where the United States could build facilities and use them with no questions asked. A number of possibilities existed, most of them under British control. The most promising was the British-owned island of Diego Garcia, located at near equi-distance (about 2000 miles) 'from all prospective operating areas'.[15]

The strategic islands concept was formally posed to Admiral Burke in June 1960. In a memorandum entitled 'Assuring a Future Base Structure in the African Indian Ocean Area', the Long-Range Objectives Group noted the possibility of 'war and tension situations' in the 'Indian Ocean, sub-Saharan African area' during the next ten to fifteen years. At the same time, Western base rights would become increasingly insecure. Only small, sparsely populated islands could safely be held 'under the full control of the West in face of the currents of nationalism'. Prompt action should be taken to segregate these territories from larger political units due for independence. This was particularly important in the case of Diego Garcia, 'a large atoll ideally suited to be the primary Western fleet base and air staging position in the Indian Ocean'. Other Islands (including Aldabra) were mentioned as possible links in a strategic chain stretching from Ascension in the South Atlantic through various points in the Indian Ocean to Australia, and thence to Subic Bay in the Philippines.[16]

Admiral Burke did not require much convincing: he began to clear the proposal with the Joint Chiefs of Staff and other Pentagon authorities. In time, it would reach the Department of State, where limited war doctrines had gained strong adherence.

THE CRISIS DEEPENS

As the 1960s progressed, military policy makers saw nothing to warrant a change of view. Decolonisation proceeded on an irresistable course; and the Western strategic position continued to slip against a background of rampant violence. Egypt and Saudi Arabia locked horns over Yemen. China and India fought a border war. Indonesia contested Malaysia's hold on Borneo. Israel triumphed in the 1967 Six-Day War, but at the cost of embarrassing US relations with friendly Arab governments. While many states on the Indian Ocean periphery seemed increasingly hostile to Western interests, there was cause as well to worry over the stability of American friends and allies. As the Commander in Chief of US Naval Forces in Europe put it:

> The entire area of Africa, Middle East, India, and the SEA peninsula is emotionally supercharged over issues of anti-colonialism, independence, Communism, neutrality, oil, wealth, extreme poverty [and] nuclear free zones.[17]

And just as naval planners feared, political difficulties created repeated uncertainty for US forces in the Indian Ocean, Africa and the Persian Gulf. In the early 1960s, a military air command plane was stranded in Africa because it could not get landing rights farther east. When the attack carrier USS *Franklin Roosevelt* transited the Indian Ocean on the way from the Atlantic to duty with the Seventh Fleet, it could only refuel in South Africa, a pariah state. A subsequent carrier transit avoided similar embarrassment only through the 'fortuitous' availability of a Royal Navy oiler. The USS *Boxer*'s cruise from Norfolk to Vietnam involved a surreptitious passage through the Suez Canal because of anti-American sentiment in the UAR. It could not refuel at Aden due to political turmoil and labour strikes. When the Joint Chiefs ordered two EA–3B aircraft transferred from Spain to Japan, the pilots ended up by spending twenty-five days en route and required numerous messages and phone calls to arrange overflight permission and logistics support.

The 1967 Arab–Israeli War compounded Washington's strategic dilemma. A small US carrier just barely slipped through the Suez Canal before it closed. With the Canal no longer serviceable, US warships in the Mediterranean had no ready access to the Persian Gulf. Even if the Canal were open, use of it could not be assured in times of crisis.[18] The diplomatic repercussions of the war were perhaps more troublesome. As the Navy remarked: 'The ports of Assab and Massawa were the only ones in the Red Sea and/or Persian Gulf other then Djibouti that were available to the US during the Arab–Israeli War of June 1967.'[19]

In sum, US military operations in the Indian Ocean were becoming increasingly chancy. The ability of US vessels even to transit the Indian Ocean – not to speak of maintaining a combat capability in, say, the Persian Gulf – depended on 'increasingly unsatisfactory makeshift arrangements'.[20]

In the view of naval planners, such 'makeshift arrangements' were all the newly independent peripheral nations could be expected to grant. For highly nationalistic ex-colonies would prove hypersensitive to foreign activities on their soil. 'The self-perceived interests of most nations in the area will not be similar to those of the US with sufficient consistency to assure that US bases, if available at all, will remain usable in times of stress on terms compatible with US interests.'[21] Again, it was national independence that posed the strategic problem, reinforcing US antagonism toward Third World 'extremism'.

But what of traditional states who might line up with the United States to secure protection against their radical neighbours? Here was an opportunity, but not one US planners saw as particularly promising. Haile Selassi had been a good friend, but he was an old man, and the future status of Ethiopia 'when the Emperor passes from the scene is quite uncertain'.[22] The Sultanates of Muscat and Oman afforded another possibility for co-operation. The British already had a facility on Masirah Island, which the US might develop for patrolling the Arabian Sea. But the Sultanate was due for change. While firmly entrenched in the Middle Ages, the Oman regime might not withstand the forces of secularism and modernisation that would surely follow the exploitation of Omani oil reserves.

And if the sultan were undone by the stresses of modernisation, he would not be alone. The 'radical' Arab states would suffer greatly from a growing gap between expectations and performance, forcing national leaders to seek external diversions to mollify their restive publics. Likewise, states in Eastern Africa confronted enormous problems of economic development, national integration and governmental capacity. 'Combined, these problems reflect the fundamental issue affecting the area as a whole – adjustment to the modern world.'[23]

Finally, external power balances seemed in fact to be turning against the West, just as planners in the early 1960s had predicted. In January 1968, fiscal difficulties at last forced the British to announce their withdrawal from 'East of Suez' by the end of 1971. The Soviets had in the meantime sent naval vessels into the Indian Ocean (in 1968) and were expanding their capacities for long-range operations. As before, this would not give the Soviets an ability to act as an imperialist power per se. But, in conjunction with increased trade and diplomatic ties, it would help them to support internal dissidents' movements and promote the radicalisation of inherently unstable littoral regimes.[24]

Thus were sounded constant themes of US Indian Ocean policy from the late 1950s to the present day. The West, with its vital stake in Persian Gulf oil, was threatened by local extremisms which the Soviets might exploit. Washington policy makers sought to contain these extremisms through a military presence that they knew would exacerbate hypersensitive nationalisms. To break out of this vicious circle, naval planners sought to diminish US reliance on mainland bases. The 'strategic island' would help compensate for colonial bastions that were now forever lost.

3 Kennedy, the Arabs and the Navy's New Frontier

John F. Kennedy and the men around him were keen to face the challenges of the post-colonial era. As a presidential candidate, Kennedy had denounced Eisenhower's supposedly lethargic response to world historical movements in Africa, Asia and Latin America. Because of Republican torpor, he declared, freedom was everywhere under attack, and unless America did much more, 'then freedom fails'. The New Frontier policy makers who took office in January 1961 were men in a hurry, eager to turn the tide of events before it was too late.

Kennedy's attack on Eisenhower proceeded along two separate lines. First, he upbraided Eisenhower for failing to align America with nationalist movements and for not acting to meet the real problems of the developing world. Second, he criticised the Republican administration for its military cost-cutting programme that left America unprepared to fight limited wars in the 'gray areas' of the Third World.

As a Senator, Kennedy advocated sweeping 'the Western house . . . clean of its own lingering imperialism'.[1] For in 'Asia, Latin America, and particularly in Africa, man's eternal desire to be free is rising to the fore'. America, 'the home of the Declaration of Independence should have led this nationalist revolution instead of helping to throttle it'.[2] The United States, he said, had to 'redouble its efforts to earn the respect of Nationalist leaders'.[3]

Kennedy was particularly severe in his criticisms of Eisenhower's Middle East policy. Washington should not, he said, delude itself into underestimating 'the cutting force of Arab nationalism or to hope to create puppet regimes or pocket Western kingdoms in the area'.[4] Repressive measures 'had only fanned the flames of discontent, and the close ties between this nation . . . and the great colonial powers' had caused Arabs to 'regard America as a supporter of colonialism'.[5] Moreover, US policy makers had in Kennedy's view made a big mistake in dealing with the Middle East in the context of East–West struggle. The real issues there were nationalism, economic development, the Arab refugees and local political instabilities. The Eisenhower Doctrine did nothing to address these problems. 'It offers guns and money, but guns and money are not the Middle East's basic need.'[6]

Kennedy's military critique of Eisenhower stood in sharp contrast to the sentiments described above. By relying on nuclear deterrence to prevent war, Kennedy charged, the Eisenhower administration had presided over the 'steady deterioration of our ability to fight local brush-fire wars'.[7] As a result, the Russians or Chinese, 'using satellites or guerrillas where possible, will continue to nibble away at our periphery'.[8] To meet this danger, the United States had to 'regain the ability to intervene effectively anywhere in the world – augmenting, modernizing and providing increased mobility and versatility for the conventional forces and weapons of the army and marine corps.'[9]

Kennedy did not explain how he intended to reconcile stepped-up military intervention 'anywhere in the world' with his posture of sympathetic understanding toward Third World nationalism. Hence, there was an unresolved inconsistency to Kennedy's rhetoric. On the one hand, he castigated Eisenhower for pursuing policies of repression – for trying to throttle the nationalist revolution. On the other hand, in a polemical about-face, he charged that Eisenhower had let American repressive capacities deteriorate.

On both scores – Eisenhower's opposition to nationalism and his supposed neglect of military strength – Kennedy's critique was overwrought. Eisenhower had understood the power of nationalism but, under the circumstances, had been unable to devise a practical formula for modus vivendi. Nor had Eisenhower neglected military power. After all, he sent Marines to Lebanon, making an efficient use of force toward political ends. More to the point, the British maintained an effective military sway over the Persian Gulf. So long as the British were there, underpinning pro-Western stability in the area, an American presence was superfluous.

In fact, Kennedy was possessed by the same ambivalences that afflicted Eisenhower. The main difference between the two men was that the contradictory strains of policy stood in sharper contrast in Kennedy's case. For the irony of Kennedy's brief tenure was that while he felt far stronger sympathies for Third World nationalism than Eisenhower, the new president was even more strongly committed to preserving the Western position through military force – and was willing to pay a much higher price to do so.

In the end, the repressive, interventionist strain of policy would overshadow the reforming, accommodationist elements of the Kennedy world view. Moreover, in accordance with their military–strategic emphasis, New Frontier officials would see the Indian Ocean as a critical theatre for US activism. They would prepare the ground for a strategy and commitment that would come to full realisation twenty years later.

WASHINGTON TRIES TO ACCOMMODATE THE ARABS

The conciliatory aspect of Kennedy's policy was directed toward two objects: settlement of the Palestinian refugee problem and rapprochement with Nasser. Neither object would be achieved – in the first instance, because US ideas for a reasonable settlement were unacceptable to the Arab side; in the second, because it proved impossible to accommodate Nasser's pan-Arabism without sacrificing US links to its conservative friends in the Middle East.

On 11 May 1961 Kennedy sent a letter to five Arab leaders (President Nasser of the UAR, King Hussein of Jordan, President Chehab of Lebanon, Premier Kassem of Iraq and King Saud of Saudi Arabia). He referred to the emergence of independent Arab states, 'respected as sovereign equals in the international community', and pledged 'every appropriate assistance' to such states 'determined to control their own destiny and to enhance the prosperity of their people'. He pledged furthermore to help resolve the Palestinian issue on the basis of repatriation or compensation for loss of property. The United States, he promised, would use its influence as a member of the Palestine Conciliation Commission (a UN body) to promote a 'just and peaceful solution' in which 'the best interest and welfare of all the Arab refugees of Palestine may be protected and advanced'.[10]

Yet Kennedy had no workable programme to obtain his ends. To his way of thinking, the refugee problem would best be solved by relocating the refugees in sparsely populated Arab states that needed new manpower and the 'hand of the cultivator'. He felt that Syria and Iraq were likely candidates in such regard. He believed the United States should help the relocation by providing money for land and water projects in Arab countries. The refugees would be compensated for lost property by Israel, with American aid. He felt that Israel could also contribute by repatriating a number of refugees. He stipulated, however, that the number could not be large: 'Israel cannot accept a great number of refugees as she is crowded into a small strip of land and has not inconsiderable absorption problems herself.'[11]

Kennedy had too much faith in economic development as a panacea for the refugee issue. He did not pay sufficient attention to the fact that the Arab states did not want to absorb the Palestinians. Neither did he consider what the Palestinians thought about the matter. He was left with a programme that accorded closely with Israeli views, but which would never be accepted by Arab governments.[12]

In addition, rather than dealing directly with the Palestinian problem, Kennedy decided to work through the UN. He got nowhere with this oblique approach. An eighteen-month mediation effort, made in 1962–3 by Dr Joseph Johnson, a Special Envoy for the Palestine Conciliation Commission, yielded no results. Johnson's proposed compromise – which was similar to Kennedy's thinking – was turned down by the Arabs amid recriminations about pro-Israeli bias on the Commission.[13]

The President's efforts to woo Nasser were more serious business than his tentative moves on behalf of the refugees. Kennedy was determined not to let the Soviet Union gain influence in the Third World through American default. In Kennedy's eyes, rapprochement with Nasser was important not only in terms of the Western position in the Middle East, but also in terms of a global political balance in which Third World nations would carry the deciding weight.

Kennedy launched his campaign to win over Nasser by appointing an Ambassador to Egypt, Dr John Badeau, former President of the American University in Cairo, who had lived in Arab countries for roughly thirty years. The president carried on a close personal correspondence with Nasser (covering a gamut of topics from Cuba to Africa to the Middle East), and made the special gesture of receiving the Egyptian Ambassador at the White House in May 1961. As an extension of his personal diplomacy, he sent Chester Bowles, the Special Presidential Representative for Asian, African and Latin American Affairs, to Cairo in February 1962. Bowles concluded from his visit that Egyptian leaders were 'pragmatists searching for techniques that will enable them to expand their economy rapidly and maintain their political grip'. He reported scepticism toward Soviet and Chinese 'economic and political concepts'. He felt that Nasser was willing to compromise, and that with 'wise policies there is a reasonable chance that we can modify Egyptian hostility and gradually turn the country into a more constructive force'.[14]

Economic assistance provided Kennedy's chief tool for gaining Nasser's favour. Kennedy began by renewing the PL 480 food programme in September 1961. He accepted recommendations that this programme be put on a multi-year basis to facilitate Egypt's development planning. During his three years in office, about twice as much aid ($500 million, mostly surplus foodstuffs) flowed to Egypt as during the fifteen-year period from 1946 to 1961.[15]

In late 1962, however, the rapprochement started to falter. In September, only days after the medieval monarchy of the Yemen was overthrown, Nasser recognised the new republican regime, and in mid-October, after the Saudis and Jordanians began assisting the royalists, sent troops to prop it up. The Yemen thus became the scene not only of a civil war, but of a struggle between Egypt and Arab monarchies. The intervention of these two sides in the Yemen conflict made it difficult for Kennedy to reconcile friendship toward Nasser with support for America's traditional allies in the region.

Kennedy tried, unsuccessfully, to straddle the fence. He recognised the Yemeni Republican government and refused to cut off aid to Egypt. But in October 1962 he also assured Riyadh of American support 'for the maintenance of Saudi Arabia's integrity'.[16] He subsequently reinforced the small US flotilla based in Bahrain – two destroyers arrived at the Saudi port of Jedda in mid-January 1963 – and agreed to station a fighter squadron on Saudi soil.

Kennedy's fence straddling was quickly assuming the nature of open backing for Washington's conservative 'friends'. Moreover, his efforts to mediate a settlement only nurtured his growing distrust of Nasser. On 17 November 1963, the President sent an identical letter to Nasser, Hussein, Prince Faisal of Saudi Arabia and President Salal of the Yemen.[17] Kennedy proposed a phased withdrawal of Egyptian troops linked to an end of external assistance to the royalists. All five agreed in principle, but the arrangement was impossible to implement. Nasser was trapped in a situation where he could not effect a premature withdrawal without severe loss of face. On their side, the Saudis felt that the royalists were winning the war and had little reason to co-operate with Kennedy. And even if the Saudis did live up to their part of the bargain in order to give Egypt time to withdraw, it would be easier, and less obtrusive, for them to resume aid to the royalists than it would be for Nasser to send Egyptian troops back to the Yemen. But Kennedy was insensitive to Nasser's predicament. In his last letter to Nasser, he took Egypt to task for failing 'to carry out its part of the Yemen disengagement agreement'. How could he have leverage with Faisal, Kennedy complained, 'when having carried out his end of the bargain, he continued to see Egyptian troops in Yemen and hear expressions of United Arab Republic government hostility from Cairo?'[18]

KENNEDY'S LEGACY

The president's accusatory letter did not sit well with Nasser. It is open to speculation whether the worsening in US–Egyptian relations could have been reversed had Kennedy lived. Apart from the Yemen affair, US–Egyptian relations had started to sour over the US decision, announced on 26 September 1963, to sell Hawk anti-aircraft missiles to Israel. Kennedy had been at pains to inform Nasser of the decision in advance, but when US newspaper reports circulated to the effect that Nasser had been consulted, Nasser felt that Kennedy's gesture had been a trick to make it look as if Egypt had tacitly accepted the sale.[19]

Thus the president's conciliatory policy ended as little more than a footnote to history. But his military strategy endured – and constitutes his chief contribution to the development of the future US position in the Middle East. That position would hinge not on America's ability to achieve a modus vivendi with Arab nationalism, or to broker political settlements to regional conflict, but on US military power in the Indian Ocean.

As formulated by New Frontier foreign policy planners, US strategy involved three main actions on the part of the United States: first, the establishment of a US presence through deployment of naval task forces in the Indian Ocean on a regular basis. Second, US aid to a financially weakened British government to keep it militarily committed 'East of Suez'; and third, just as the Navy had proposed, acquisition of island bases to support military actions – including invervention ashore – in Southeast Asia, Eastern Africa and the Persian Gulf.

THE US PRESENCE

We have already noted Admiral Arleigh Burke's early advocacy of an Indian Ocean fleet. To create this fleet, he even contemplated (albeit reluctantly) reductions in the Mediterranean and Pacific. We have also seen that he wasted little time in approaching the Secretary of the Navy, John B. Connally, with his ideas – which fell now on attentive ears. For the president's campaign talk was not mere rhetoric. He took a strong interest not only in Third World affairs, but in forces, weapons and strategic doctrines. Indeed, he played a direct role in committing US power to the Indian Ocean.

As noted above, when hostilities threatened between the United Arab Republic and Saudi Arabia in 1963, Kennedy ordered the small Bahrain flotilla strengthened with two additional destroyers from the Sixth Fleet. He also sent a fighter squadron to Spain en route to Saudi Arabia. Political problems caused by this latter movement roused his interest in a US carrier presence in the Indian Ocean. As a result, he asked the Defense Department to consider carrier task force cruises as part of its strategic planning for the area. While subsequent inter-agency discussions revealed no consensus for a separate Indian Ocean fleet, periodic cruises were deemed highly desirable.

Kennedy's assassination in November 1963 brought no deflection in the course of US planning. For Lyndon Johnson managed to match his predecessor's enthusiasm for military power without, however, replicating any of Kennedy's nuanced understanding of world histori-cal movements. Thus, the idea of Indian Ocean naval deployments accorded well with Johnson's views on how to conduct foreign policy. In National Security Action Memorandum 289, dated 19 March 1964, McGeorge Bundy conveyed President Johnson's decision approving periodic deployments in the area. For starters, a so-called Concord Squadron (Secretary of State Dean Rusk's suggestion) would be sent on an Indian Ocean cruise. The Secretaries of State and Defense were instructed to submit plans for 'regular and intermittent deployments'. The first cruise took place in April and May 1964 and the second in August and September.[20]

KEEPING BRITAIN IN

No objective was more central to US Indian Ocean planning than to preserve a British presence East of Suez. Washington did not relish the thought of going it alone in a new strategic theatre; but more than that, the British commanded boundless respect for their ability to do much with limited means. British professionalism, honed by a long historical experience, made Britain the power most suited to take the lead in safeguarding Western interests in the turbulent years ahead.

It was indeed during the twilight of Britain's world power that the British appeared in most impressive form: British action in East Africa and the Persian Gulf inspired Washington policy makers in their tactical planning as well as in their sense of what could be done. American strategy was in fact modelled on three stellar examples of British 'police' work in Oman, Kuwait and East Africa. These cases demonstrated (so it seemed) both the continued efficacy of Western power and innovative ways to employ it.

In July 1957 a revolt broke out in the sultanate of Muscat and Oman. When RAF air operations failed to suppress it, the British opened a ground attack in early August, moving British combat units from Aden and Kenya and support units from Cyprus to prop up the Sultan's forces. After only ten days of British ground operations, the revolt collapsed.

The Oman affair showed the value of mobile forces operating from central reserves. The British intervention in Kuwait, a much larger operation, afforded a wider proof of how the West could retain supremacy in the face of hostile nationalisms.

On 26 June 1961, six days after Great Britain had relinquished her sixty-two year protectorate over Kuwait, Iraqi President Kassem laid claim to the now 'sovereign' nation. He asserted that Kuwait had been historically part of Iraq and that the British had detached the territory by means of a 'forged treaty'. Following reported Iraqi troop movements toward the Kuwait border, the Kuwaiti ruler, Sheik Sir Abdullah al-Salim al-Sabeh, requested British assistance.

The sheik made his request on the morning of 30 June. Within twenty-four hours the first British troops had arrived – a Royal Marine Commando (600 men) deployed from the HMS *Bulwark*, a recently converted 'commando carrier' specially designed to dispatch Royal Marine units to trouble areas and speed them ashore by helicopter. A squadron of tanks arrived on the same day, carried by two landing ships. The first RAF planes also arrived. Over the next six days reinforcements poured in by sea and air: by 7 July, 5700 British troops were in Kuwait. British air superiority was assured by the appearance two days later of the fleet carrier HMS *Victorious*.

If the Iraqis had ever entertained plans for military action, they wilted in the face of the rapid British military build-up. The British began to withdraw on 19 July. Kuwait was admitted to the Arab League the next day; and in mid-September Arab League troops from Saudi Arabia, Jordan, Tunisia and the Sudan took over from the remaining British forces.

The Kuwait action was followed in 1964 by an equally striking British success in East Africa. In January, the armies of Tanganyika, Kenya and Uganda mutinied. The three heads of government – Julius Nyerere, Jomo Kenyatta and Milton Obote – requested British help, which was swift and brilliant. Using troops airlifted from Britain and Aden, and from British naval vessels stationed off the East African coast, the British quashed the rebels in short order. In this instance, the fleet carrier HMS *Centaur* served as an improvised commando ship deploying troops to Tanganyika.

But the British would not for long operate at such heights. For both the territorial and financial bases of British power were withering away. American policy makers saw the problem clearly and struggled to resolve it. The strategic islands were critical to the resolution they would seek.

In a memorandum prepared in April of 1963, Jeffrey C. Kitchen, Director of the State Department's Bureau of Politico-Military Affairs, noted the implications of Britain's territorial retreat. 'Until about 1948,' he wrote,

> the British had full political control of a number of military bases of varying capability which provided for almost all types of military operations in the Indian Ocean area. The granting of independence to former British colonies has led to the closing of a number of these bases, such as Trincomalee in Ceylon. As remaining territories achieve independence this process may be expected to continue; Mombasa, on which the British have expended a considerable amount of money, will almost certainly be closed when Kenya achieves independence. The short-term future of Aden as a base does not inspire confidence. The long-term future of the Singapore base is unpredictable but apparently assured for the present.[21]

Current British strategy, Kitchen remarked, envisioned stationing at Aden mobile forces, which would move to trouble spots on commando carriers or transport aircraft. Anglo–American joint development of island facilities would accord with British thinking and permit their mobile forces to remain effective when the Aden base was lost.[22] This was crucial, officials thought, to US hopes for strengthening the 'overall Western military posture in the Indian Ocean'[23] with moves 'to complement (but not in any way to replace) the existing British effort in the area'.[24]

The strategic islands would serve an economic purpose as well. *Regardless* of problems arising from decolonisation and increasingly assertive nationalisms, the British economy could not withstand high levels of defence expenditure. If Britain were to remain committed, she would need financial help. An American share in the cost of constructing island facilities would subsidise the British presence, tending, as Foy Kohler noted in a December 1966 letter to Deputy

Defense Secretary Cyrus Vance, 'to keep the British physically in the area'.[25]

Yet Washington defence planners knew that they might be struggling in a losing cause. The British government, as Kohler wrote, 'will be under continuing economic stress'. As a result, 'they will always seek areas in which overseas expenditures will be reduced. . . .'[26] To be sure, the Prime Minister and his Minister of Defence, Denis Healey, wanted to retain Britain's presence East of Suez, as did the Foreign Secretary, Michael Stewart. They also decided to purchase the Polaris missile system and a US long-range fighter-bomber – the F–111. However, there was strong Cabinet sentiment for a stringent ceiling on defence spending. 'In this situation,' as Jeffrey Kitchen argued, 'a US-financed contribution to obtain the islands could provide the margin the Wilson–Stewart–Healey group need to persuade the Cabinet it is worth the candle to stay "East of Suez".'[27]

THE BRITISH INDIAN OCEAN TERRITORY

In April 1963 the State Department's Bureau of Politico-Military Affairs received formal authorisation to approach the British government on the Indian Ocean leasing scheme. The immediate objective was to prevent the inadvertent release of possible strategic sites, including Diego Garcia and Aldabra, from British control. It was vital, therefore, that both islands be detached from the parent colonies and placed under permanent British sovereignty.[28]

Before direct negotiations began, Britain had a new, Labour, government. If anything, the change was a propitious one for US policy, for, as Harold Wilson had declared on 16 December 1963,

> whatever we may do in the field of cost-effectiveness, value for money and a stringent review of expenditure, we cannot afford to relinquish our world role – our role, which, for shorthand purposes is sometimes called our 'East of Suez' role.

Britain, he continued, could never compete in the nuclear 'arithmetic of megatons'. Her future claims as a world power would rest on her 'ability to mount peacekeeping operations that no one else can mount'.[29]

Thus, when US negotiators went to London in February 1964, they were pushing on open doors. Neither party wished to station large, permanent forces in the region. But both saw the need to back up vital

Western interests with military power. The strategic islands scheme would let them have things both ways, providing logistics centres and staging posts for sea or airborne forces which would make up in mobility what they lacked in numerical strength.[30]

There were, however, differing emphases within the same strategic framework. Washington, as we have seen, was inclined toward a naval emphasis. For this reason, American negotiators had a primary interest in building facilities on Diego Garcia. If surveys confirmed US expectations, the island would support a wide range of military actions. The Navy had an *immediate* need for a communications centre. But over the long term, more extensive development was contemplated. Harbour dredging would provide anchorage for 'a carrier task force, [and] amphibious and support ships'.[31] Fuel, equipment and ammunition might be prestocked (either on the ground or on 'floating depots') for subsequent 'marrying with mobile combat units which might be deployed into the area'.[32] Such stockpiles could supply 'a substantial portion of an army division. . . An airbase might support cargo, carrier, and tanker aircraft.'[33] Aerial surveillance, anti-submarine patrols and air logistics operations could be conducted from such a base. All this accorded completely with the 1960s attitude that US forces should be able to go anywhere and do anything to maintain 'stability' in the world.[34]

London, despite the success of commando carrier operations (and after a bitter inter-service wrangle between the Royal Navy and the RAF), emphasised airborne interventions. British planners, therefore, saw Aldabra, an island off the East African coast, as crucial to their efforts there. Indeed, in subsequent discussions, Denis Healey pressed this view on McNamara,[35] whose role throughout the strategic islands planning was that of reluctant dragon. In the British scheme, Aldabra would afford a staging ground to airlift troops and supplies into Africa. Long-range fighter-bombers, also stationed on Aldabra, would provide tactical air support.

Rather than conflicting, the differing emphases reinforced US hopes for assuring joint responsibility. In particular, East Africa was considered a realm for continued British 'leadership'.[36] This meeting of minds was hardly coincidental. US and British naval personnel talked with each other frequently through military channels. More important, US embassy officials and their Foreign Office counterparts conversed about strategic concepts in numerous informal settings. The Royal Air Force had already formulated a strategic island scheme of its own, in which Aldabra would be a link. And McNamara, the reluctant dragon, became less reluctant when assured that Aldabra and Diego Garcia would not give the Navy another ocean for a full-fledged fleet. Moreover, he wanted Britain to go through on its intention to buy F–111s. He was concerned that without somewhere to base them and something for them to do, the rationale for the purchase would vanish. Aldabra could be the needed 'somewhere', and East African interventions might give them something to do.

The two countries agreed then to conduct joint surveys of selected islands under British control to determine which ones would prove the most promising as strategic redoubts. It was taken for granted that Diego Garcia and Aldabra would end high on the list. There were further understandings that Britain would then detach the strategic islands from the Mauritius and Seychelles administrations. The cost of the detachment would be a main British contribution to the common programme. The United States would assume the full burden of construction on Diego Garcia and would share construction costs on Aldabra. The resulting bases would be available for joint use.[37]

But before these plans took effect, two things had to happen. First, the detachments would have to take place. There was no doubt that they would – but there was considerable handwringing over how to do this while at once minimising the anticipated Third World outcry over Anglo–American 'neo-colonialism'. Second, the facilities would have to be funded. Here, Robert McNamara would display acute ambivalence. With his control of the Pentagon budget he could frustrate any State Department understandings which involved military spending – and in the case of the Indian Ocean basing scheme, he did so.

THE STRATEGIC ISLANDS AND THE THIRD WORLD

US officials harboured no delusions about Third World reaction to the island bases. To be sure, several countries would welcome an increased US presence. Yet in others, the proposed actions would 'provoke suspicion and criticism' the Chinese might exploit. The critics, moreover, would prove 'more vocal than the supporters'.[38] And in the UN, the general atmosphere, 'including Afro–Asian anti-colonial and anti-base sentiment, as well as Communist propaganda efforts', would be poor.[39]

Washington had already had a foretaste of Third World displeasure before the first Concord Squadron visited the Indian Ocean. American officials had hoped that India would approve of the US naval presence.

In late 1963 careful steps were taken to inform the Indian government of the pending move. General Maxwell D. Taylor was sent to New Delhi in mid-December to discuss the issue with Prime Minister Nehru. The first Indian responses augured well. India had fought a border war with China in 1962 and seemed well-disposed toward American arguments that the proposed naval deployment would help defeat the 'Chicom threat in Asia'. The Indian government was expected to present no big problem: press and popular reaction was the chief concern. This expectation seemed to be borne out. When an American news leak about the Indian Ocean task force stirred a political tempest in India, the Indian ambassador came to the State Department to express regrets over the 'press flurry'. If the US could not control it, he lamented, 'something very desirable may get interfered with'.[40] The prime minister himself gave cause for optimism. Speaking in the parliament after his meeting with General Taylor, he declared that 'India could not object to anyone going on high seas wherever they liked'.[41]

It came as some surprise, then, when the Indian ambassador in Washington deflated US hopes in a sudden volte-face. If India had been consulted on the proposed Indian Ocean deployment, he said, she would have advised against it. It would not be welcomed by non-aligned countries. Already, Chinese propagandists had seized on the 'crude press play' to charge that India had moved away from non-alignment – an argument especially damaging to the Indian position in Africa 'where unsophisticated governments' were susceptible to the Chinese ploy. The US naval presence would serve no useful purpose, he declared. It would only damage America's reputation among non-aligned countries in Africa and Asia.[42]

These warnings went unheeded: Washington planners were determined to augment Western strength in the area despite local views. As in the case of US naval cruises, no one expected to win widespread approval of the basing scheme by Third World states. The best that could be done was to minimise embarrassment. This, officials felt, might be accomplished with good tactics and the right timing. In the meanwhile, as the survey and detachment proceedings were underway, the strategic islands scheme would be 'closely held'.[43]

But US planners did not count on an enterprising *Washington Post* reporter, Robert Estabrook. In June 1964, Estabrook filed a story on the Anglo–American island bases. Not only did his story divulge information the State Department wanted to withhold from Third World governments, but he had managed to capture in precise detail the strategic *zeitgeist* underlying the whole venture, including the use of the islands 'as potential air and sea bases and as staging areas for the airlift of troops to trouble areas'.

State Department officials met with *Post* managing editor Alfred Friendly to try to quash the story. They argued that publication would complicate British negotiations with the Mauritius and Seychelles authorities who had not yet been informed of the base initiative. Also, conversations would be more difficult if 'conducted in the glare [of] Communist and neutralist propaganda'.[44] They apprised him as well of the UN situation. Friendly agreed to stop publication, provided the *Post* was given advance notice when the American and British governments were ready to release the information officially. In case a leak did occur, Washington cabled instructions to the London embassy on what to say in response. If mention were made of Indian Ocean bases, the appropriate reply would be that the US and Britain had been holding discussions concerning the building of a US radio communications station. If more exposition were needed, then spokesmen might admit that 'some other facilities' were being considered 'over the long-term'.[45]

The Department had no chance to test these circumlocutions. In August, a leak developed in London which led both the *Post* and the *Cleveland Plain Dealer* to publish the full story before a competitor did. The basing scheme, replete with its interventionist overtones, was no longer secret. And Third World reaction to it proved the accuracy of earlier predictions. As one official noted:

> Press reaction in Pakistan, India, Afghanistan, and Mauritius, among others has by and large been in opposition to a U.S./U.K. military presence in the Indian Ocean. Our mission to the UN has warned of difficulties. . . Communist and Afro–Asian bloc countries will undoubtedly generate opposition in the UN and elsewhere. The final communiqué of a recent Cairo non-aligned conference included condemnation of the 'expressed intention of the imperialist powers to establish bases in the Indian Ocean'.[46]

But secrecy was not the only weapon by which Washington sought top dampen Third World anti-colonial sentiment. A great premium was placed on timing. Prior to formal discussions with the British, US policy makers were concerned with the speed of action. Quick action might 'minimize the possibility that local populations would come under external pressures for self-determination or be an object of concern to the UN'. Also, by doing as much as possible before the

September 1964 meeting of the UN colonialism subcommittee (the 'Committee of 24') anti-Western pressure might be relieved. This committee, dominated by Afro–Asian countries, had already called for Britain to liquidate its base at Aden. It was part of a hostile UN atmosphere that vexed Washington and was seen as favouring Soviet interests.[47]

The British, however, moved more slowly than the State Department wished, putting as they did considerably more stress on securing local concurrence than US policy makers – who feared the British might concede a veto to the Mauritian Prime Minister – thought appropriate. They waited until June 1965 (nearly a year after the surveys were complete) before they agreed to detach the Chagos Archipelago (the larger group containing Diego Garcia) from Mauritius, and Aldabra, Farquhar and Ile des Roches from the Seychelles. In order to temper Third World criticism, they took steps to get the Mauritius and Seychelles governments to approve the detachment. Tentative soundings to these governments revealed that the 'enabling' costs would involve a $28 million payout. Secretary McNamara agreed to assume half the burden, deducting up to $14 million in research and development costs due to the United States under the 1963 Polaris sales agreement with Great Britain.[48]

In September 1965, the Cabinet decided formally on the detachment. Prime Minister Wilson presented this decision as part of a package deal to the Prime Minister of Mauritius, then in London for a constitutional conference on the future of his country. Along with detachment of the Chagos Archipelago, the package included a British defence arrangement with Mauritius, independence within a year, and a large financial 'contribution'.[49]

On 8 November 1965, the Queen issued an Order in Council that formed a 'British Indian Ocean Territory' (BIOT) consisting of the Chagos Archipelago, the Farquhar Islands, the Aldabra Group, and Des Roches. The order came at a propitious time for Anglo–American planners concerned with Third World sensibilities. At the end of October, the British government had made a last ditch attempt to negotiate a settlement to the Southern Rhodesia question. When talks with the white regime failed, a full-scale crisis blew up in early November, culminating in the Rhodesian authorities' Unilateral Declaration of Independence (UDI) on November 11. The Queen's detachment order, coming in the midst of this crisis, was issued at a time when world attention was focused on a more salient concern – just what Britain needed to minimise anti-colonialist outcry. The British policy of moving with deliberation had paid off.

THE McNAMARA PROBLEM

As a general rule, the 1960s marked a period of Pentagon leadership in foreign policy. On most important issues, Dean Rusk deferred to McNamara. Besides, Rusk himself, along with many high level subordinates (in particular U. Alexis Johnson), was enamoured with military power and all too ready to define political problems in strategic terms. Moreover, the State Department's Bureau of Politico–Military Affairs handled Indian Ocean planning. Here, thinking was almost entirely oriented toward bases, deployments, troops, aircraft, ships and logistics. Other cultures and national histories were of interest solely for their strategic implications.

In a departure from the normal pattern, the Department of State took the lead in formulating the US response to revolutionary nationalism in the Indian Ocean region. Civilians in the Pentagon followed this lead – sometimes reluctantly, for the strategic islands scheme could provide an entrée for a permanent Indian Ocean fleet which McNamara opposed.

McNamara moved in fits and starts – not opposing the scheme completely, but constantly obstructing it. In the February 1964 discussions, the British agreed to pay all the costs of detachment. When costs doubled beyond the original estimate, they asked the US to help out. McNamara balked, even though the sum was only $14 million. At last, he grudgingly gave his consent, agreeing not to a direct payment, but to a deduction of Polaris research and development costs mentioned above. Later, when the British indicated a desire to move toward early construction on Aldabra, the most McNamara promised was that the US would 'consider' a contribution. The Secretary's parsimony vexed and confounded politico–military planners in the Department of State, who worried that US procrastination would discourage Britain and sap the scheme of vital momentum.[50]

In 1967, McNamara struck his hardest blow against the Indian Ocean base advocates. By that time, budgetary constraints arising from Vietnam weighed heavily. Also, the Aldabra project had been delayed by protests from a naturalists' lobby represented by the Royal Audubon Society and the Smithsonian Institution. Naturalists argued that a rare bird would be disturbed by air operations. Most distressing, the British now refused to participate in funding or manning a Diego Garcia facility pending resolution of the Aldabra issue.

Reserving judgement on Aldabra, McNamara would flatly reject Diego Garcia. The bureaucratic interplay that preceded this rejection gave good occasion for investigating the objectives and rationales that characterised nearly ten years of US planning for the Indian Ocean and Persian Gulf areas: the political problem of rising nationalism was cast once more in strategic terms, and to cope with it US policy makers looked toward military options.

In February 1967, the Navy forwarded a request for $26 million to build an 'austere support facility' on Diego Garcia, regardless of whether the British chose to participate in its funding or use. The Navy's memorandum, drawn up in the Navy Department's Systems Analysis Branch under the direction of Admiral Elmo Zumwalt, who later capped his career with appointment as Richard Nixon's Chief of Naval Operations, couched the argument for the base in the lexicon of cost-effectiveness: with an anchorage and fuel stockpile on Diego Garcia, carrier task forces could transit the Indian Ocean more cheaply compared with the costs of refuelling by tanker.[51]

In June 1967, the Assistant Secretary of Defense for International Security Affairs (ISA) requested the views of the Joint Chiefs of Staff on the Diego Garcia proposal. The Chiefs' memorandum, dated 25 July 1967, departed from the narrow technical arguments employed by the Navy's systems analysts. Rather, the document laid out a comprehensive strategic rationale which reflected not only many years of official thinking about the Indian Ocean, but also the world view of the globalist era of US foreign policy. 'US strategic interests in the area', the Chiefs asserted, 'are important and will increase in the future'. One of the chief such interests was oil. A high percentage of Western European oil needs were filled by Middle Eastern supplies. 'While other suppliers are more important to the United States, their ability in turn depends on continued free access of Western Europe to Middle Eastern oil,' Added to this supreme interest was the need to live up to treaty commitments to Pakistan, Iran, Thailand and Australia. Moreover, the United States had important military installations in Ethiopia and Saudi Arabia, and others in South Africa and Malagasy, and it had to be ready to encourage other friendly states.

These interests were seen as subject to increasing peril. Prior to the First World War, European nations were 'primarily responsible for the peace of the Indian Ocean area', but now only Great Britain remained in strength – little comfort because she 'had been rapidly disengaging . . . for the past dozen years'. 'The result', the memorandum pointed out, 'has been the emergence of numerous weak and mutually antagonistic states who are suspicious, to varying degrees, or openly hostile to their formerly colonial rulers and to Western states in general.' The Soviets and Chinese were taking advantage of these internal instabilities to cultivate influence with Arab and African countries.

No mention was made in the memorandum of a direct Soviet threat to the region. Thus, as before, the strategic problem depicted here arose from uncontrollable nationalisms the Communist powers might exploit. The logical conclusion to be drawn from this line of thought was that to protect Western interests from Soviet designs, the United States would have to control internal changes in weak, inchoate polities and act as regional gendarme, policing disputes between them.

In the JCS view, existing United States capabilities were insufficient to deal with prospective events in the area. The only assured facilities were owned by Britain, and these were rapidly diminishing. A case in point was the Aden base: during the 1967 Arab–Israeli crisis, strikes, lockouts, work slowdowns and terrorism made the port unavailable for refuelling and indeed, according to the report of the American consul, put the entire base in jeopardy.

Without the Diego Garcia base, the Chiefs continued, military options in the Indian Ocean and Persian Gulf theatres would be exceedingly limited. And haste was of the essence: the Soviet Union and some Afro–Asian states were attempting to create a political situation that would foreclose utilisation of the British Indian Ocean Territory islands. The UN Committee of 24 had already charged the US and Great Britain with neo-colonialism, and members of the Indian Parliament had raised vehement opposition to Western bases in the Indian Ocean. These efforts were not likely to decrease with time. In order to provide the necessary facilities to support military power in the region, the United States had therefore to act quickly to avoid paying an even higher political price for their development.

As for the base itself, the Chiefs envisioned a multi-purpose staging area to support US military action throughout the littoral. The $26 million facility proposed by the Navy could provide a basis for massive movements of US forces into the region in 'contingency situations'. Moreover, although 'the initial project would be primarily a naval facility, the bulk of investment would provide improvements of a general purpose nature which could be developed further to meet additional future requirements' – such as air force operations. The memorandum provided a list of situations in which US military power might be deployed from a Diego Garcia staging post. Twenty possibilities were listed – all comprising internal and regional crises, none involving Soviet military action in the area. Disturbances in

India, political unrest in Ceylon, secession of East Pakistan from West Pakistan, an Iraqi attack on Kuwait or Iran, hostilities between Ethiopia and Somalia, and between Somalia and Kenya, domestic upheaval in Ethiopia – these and more were presented as cases requiring US interventionist capabilities in the Indian Ocean.[52]

We can question, of course, the seriousness of the JCS document: it is not uncommon to inflate rationales in order to secure programme funding. But when judged within the context of how US policy evolved over a long period of time, the JCS memorandum takes on added gravity. Indeed, in the eyes of Admiral Zumwalt, who had overseen preparation of the Navy's cost-effectiveness rationale of February, it was the systems analysis argument that lacked seriousness. He had commissioned it only because McNamara was numbers-oriented and thus ill at ease with broad strategic concepts. By speaking McNamara's own language in respect to Diego Garcia, Zumwalt hoped to overcome the Secretary's mental barriers and gain approval for the Indian Ocean base. But for Zumwalt, the cost-effectiveness justification was nothing short of foolish.

But even Zumwalt's cost-effectiveness packaging of a Diego Garcia proposal was unavailing in 1967. Consumed in the Vietnam nightmare, McNamara had become increasingly resistant to military pestering for added US bases and commitments. He had already testified before Congress on the futility of the American bombing campaign, thus ensuring the wrath of President Johnson. In the case of the Indian Ocean 'support facility', the Asia division in the Office of the Assistant Secretary of Defense for Systems Analysis gave McNamara the reason he apparently wanted to disapprove its funding. Pointing out that the Navy had left ceratin costs out of account – neglecting to calculate the expense of diverting ships to Diego Garcia to take on fuel – the civilian analysts shredded the Navy's cost-effectiveness calculations. They also took issue with the political assumptions underlying US expansion into the Indian Ocean. The United States, in their view, would not wish to become involved unilaterally in South Asia where local bases were denied. If assistance were requested, then nations requesting such assistance would grant base rights, thus obviating the need for Diego Garcia. Third World political reaction to an Indian Ocean base had already heated up. And the original motivation for developing the facility – to work jointly with the British – had disappeared with Britain's refusal to join in. Finally, 'one would hope we could avoid a race with Peking and Moscow to develop military capabilities in the Indian Ocean area, perhaps in the same way we are attempting to avoid an ABM race, by not giving the other side a reason for acting'. The systems analysis evaluation was the final stage in the approval process of the McNamara Pentagon. Not only did these negative conclusions regarding Diego Garcia reflect McNamara's own disillusionment with military interventionism, but they were the last argument, and were thus placed, along with a letter of transmittal, on the top of the file which reached the Secretary. In a memorandum of 27 October 1967, McNamara accepted the systems analysis position and rejected the Navy's proposal.[53]

But the bureaucratic momentum was only slowed. The next year McNamara had left as Defense Secretary, replaced by Clark Clifford. Paul Nitze, the Secretary of the Navy during the first try at approval, was now Assistant Secretary of Defense, thus guaranteeing that the project would be accepted. The base was renamed an 'austere communications facility' and was presented as an 'Option B' – a middle ground between Option A (doing nothing) and Option C, a more grandiose scheme costing $55 million.[54] With this repackaging, the proposal succeeded. In 1968 the British began the unpleasant task of deporting the 1000 residents of the Chagos Group and dumping them in Mauritius.[55] US Navy Seabees arrived in March 1971; and up until the Middle East war of 1973, over $40 million had been spent on the 'communications facility'.

WAR AGAIN – ISRAEL'S 1967 VICTORY AND THE AFTERMATH

The Navy had secured its foothold in the Indian Ocean. Little noticed at the time, the Navy's bureaucratic victory had a long-run significance few could have predicted. Its importance in the overall working of US Middle East policy was overshadowed by explosive developments on the Arab–Israeli front – where the United States was oddly passive toward the movement of events. Yet the passivity itself represented something of a fateful choice.

After the souring of Kennedy's brief rapprochement with Nasser, the President's assassination ended any possibility for restoring the US–Egyptian dialogue. Lyndon Johnson had few of Kennedy's sensitivities toward the Third World and was disinclined to rebuild personal links with Nasser. Indeed, communication between Washington and Cairo took on unpleasant undertones. In one cable to the US Embassy in Cairo, for example, the American Ambassador was instructed to make Nasser 'completely understand' that Western military facilities in the region (viz. the US Air Force base in Libya and the British naval base at Aden) were part of a 'Free World defense' that provided non-aligned states a 'free ride'. Egypt's opposition to such bases, the cable implied, resembled 'communist efforts' to eliminate Western bases necessary to the 'survival of the Free World'. If such an identity between the Egyptian and communist positions were a calculated feature of Cairo policy, then 'we would ask if this is not [a] change in UAR policy of non-alignment as we understand it'.[56]

When Arab–Israeli tension once more reached the boiling point in May 1967, Johnson was not disposed to exert his full influence to keep Israel from dealing a hard blow to the Arabs. To begin with, his main attention was on the costly débâcle in Vietnam. Besides, to Johnson's way of thinking, Nasser had forced confrontation. On 14 May 1967, the Egyptian leader had sent forces into the Sinai Peninsula. He then demanded the removal of United Nations Emergency Force troops from the Egyptian–Israeli border area, and following their withdrawal, announced the closure of the Strait of Tiran to Israeli shipping.

Israel struck early in the morning of 5 June, destroying Egypt's air force on the ground in a superbly executed surprise attack. By the cessation of hostilities on June 10, Israel had thoroughly routed Egyptian, Syrian and Jordanian forces, and had conquered a territory around double the size of Israel itself: the Sinai Peninsula, the Gaza Strip, the Jordanian West Bank and the Golan Heights of Syria – all were under Israeli occupation.

Johnson's response to the new situation set the stage for years to come. He did not seem to care that Nasser's buildup in the Sinai followed an Israeli threat, made on May 12, of retaliation against Syria for raids into northern Israel by Syrian equipped Palestinian guerrillas. Nor did the President seem to care about the political difficulties Nasser would have faced if he appeared indifferent to threatened Israeli action against Syria. The fact that no evidence existed of any actual Egyptian intention to attack was likewise irrelevant to Johnson's thinking. Most of all, he did not analyse the war, and the events leading up to it, in the overall context of the Arab–Israeli conflict. Hence, unlike Eisenhower or Kennedy, he was not interested in pursuing any scheme (no matter how modest) to address the basic causes of the 1967 war – and of the two prior wars. Instead, he was content to let the Arabs pay the costs of their provocations. What he wanted above all was an untroubled status quo in the Middle East, so that he did not have an additional, intractable worry while he was mired in Vietnam. He would secure this status quo by making sure that Israel was so strong that the Arabs could not challenge it.

It was for this reason that Johnson got seriously into the business of supplying Israel arms. Prior to the 1967 Six-Day War, Israel received most of its arms from France. With the French refusal to continue playing that role – de Gaulle wanted now to foster closer relations with Arab states – the United States stepped into the breach. In late December 1968, a deal was concluded to provide Israel with F–4 Phantom jets. No quid pro quo was exacted. The Israelis were not asked to agree even in principle to full withdrawal from the occupied territories as part of an overall peace settlement. In effect, the United States put itself in the position of underwriting the occupation. As a short-run solution, the policy made good sense. In a not too distant future, the defects would become all too clear.

4 Nixon and his Doctrine

Richard Nixon had few ambivalences about the Third World. Unlike Eisenhower or Kennedy, Nixon was never attracted to the idea of a modus vivendi with radical nationalisms. Nor was his National Security Adviser (later Secretary of State) Henry Kissinger. For them, simple repression was the appropriate US response to currents of Third World change.

Nixon's problem, however, was that his immediate predecessor, Lyndon Johnson, was also partial to simple repression – and had pursued it *à outrance* in Vietnam. The twin results were a shattered foreign policy consensus and a failing economy, ravaged by a deficit-spawned inflation. Nixon was fettered, thus, by decreasing public support not only for the war in Vietnam, but also for an interventionist foreign policy elsewhere in the world. He was fettered as well by economic constraints: in an inflationary milieu he had to contain the growth of federal spending – and this, in Nixon's view, required substantial cutbacks on defence. The president, then, would have to support US foreign policy objectives with diminished means.

Nixon rose to the challenge in Vietnam. To relieve political and economic pressures at home he reduced the direct costs of the US commitment. The war was 'Vietnamised'. Local forces were strengthened by US weapons aid. In time, they took over an increasing share of combat operations on the ground. The United States backed them up with air power, thus economising in American money and lives. The United States remained in Vietnam – and Nixon won re-election as a peace president.

In much the same way, Nixon rose to the challenge in the Middle East. He had no intention of abandoning the area to revolutionary upheaval. But at the same time, he had no programme to realise peaceful change. Rather, he looked toward repression to stabilise the status quo.

Yet, whatever America's interest in the status quo, the shock of Vietnam made it difficult to commit US forces to its defence. Nixon would therefore 'Vietnamize' the Persian Gulf. Local powers would be equipped and trained to act in Washington's stead; the United States would provide air and sea power to back them up.

Underlying Nixon's strategy was the presupposition that the Persian Gulf was a separate theatre, connected to the Indian Ocean, but

The Arabian (Persian) Gulf

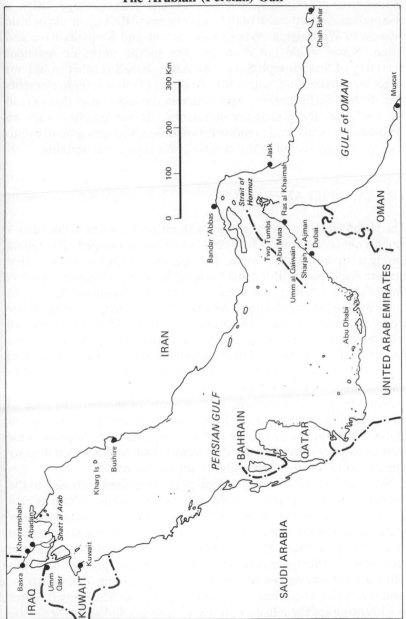

Source: Amin Saikal, *The Rise and Fall of the Shah* (Princeton: Princeton University Press, 1980).

distinct from the rest of the Middle East. Given this presupposition, a comprehensive settlement of the larger issues in the region was of little interest to Washington. Where Eisenhower and Kennedy tried and failed, Nixon would not even try. For in the words of Assistant Secretary of State Joseph Sisco, the Arab–Israeli conflict would not affect the Persian Gulf 'with quite the direct emotional tense elements as in the Middle East *per se*, in particular in those countries that were in the 1967 war, the principal combatants'.[1] It was precisely such an attitude that would lead administration officials to turn a blind eye to reality – falsely secure in the comfort of a repressive 'stability'.

THE TWO PILLARS POLICY

The Nixon Doctrine (née the 'Guam Doctrine') was first articulated – 'not for quotation' – on 25 July 1969, when Nixon stopped off in Guam during a trip around the world. The president's emphasis was at that time on Asian policy. But in his 'state of the world' report to Congress on 18 February 1970, and in subsequent reports, he put the doctrine in the context of global strategy. America, he said, would live up to her treaty commitments. But she would not (and could not) 'conceive all the plans, design all the programs, execute all the decisions, and undertake all the defense of the free nations of the world'.[2] Means had to be discovered to permit the United States to remain committed in ways it could both afford and sustain.

Nixon proposed, therefore, to turn more of the burdens over to American friends and allies. In non-nuclear conflicts, the United States would furnish economic and military assistance in accordance with its military commitments, but would 'look to the nation directly threatened to assume responsibility for its defense'.[3]

Nixon policy makers quickly applied the president's strategy to the Persian Gulf. As a result of Britain's decision to withdraw from its East of Suez presence by the end of 1971, Nixon ordered a searching review of the future US role in the Gulf. The review concluded that the United States should not take Britain's place as guardian of stability in the area. States within the region would have to assume primary responsibility for preserving peace by co-operating among themselves to ensure security and promote economic progress. The United States would encourage them to do so by expanding US diplomatic ties in the Gulf and backing them up with political and technical aid.

The policy of relying on regional powers was endorsed in subsequent studies, ordered by National Security Adviser Henry Kissinger in November and December 1970, on the Indian Ocean as a whole. They concluded that US interests would indeed be harmed if hostile forces gained influence over the region and its oil; yet, over the next five years (1971–5), US interests there would be substantially less important than in Latin America, Europe or the Far East. Soviet naval deployments were seen as cautious probes which would, in time, bring increased naval presence. But considering the general limits on US naval strength, it would not be the best use of scarce resources to increase the number of US ships in the Indian Ocean. As in the case of the Persian Gulf, the burden of preserving security in the wider Indian Ocean region would fall primarily on friendly local states.[4] For the time being, the United States could maintain a low profile.

When stripped to essentials, the Nixon strategy had one critical feature, overriding all the rest: a massive US arms transfer to the two 'key countries' in the area – Iran and Saudi Arabia.[5] These states, in the Nixon scheme, would assume the primary burden of policing the Persian Gulf. They would develop their abilities to do so by expanding and modernising their forces with high quality American weapons. This military supply policy – the linchpin of the so-called 'Twin Pillars' strategy – was, as one official pointed out, the logical extension not only of the Nixon Doctrine, but of 'longstanding defense relations in the area, centered in Iran and Saudi Arabia and going back even to World War II days'.[6]

IRAN

The shah's Iran was the most important of the twin pillars. In the unlikely event of a direct Soviet drive on the Persian Gulf, a powerful Iran would block the way long enough for external assistance to arrive. But the most probable field of action would be toward the South. There, the shah would 'ensure the vital oil routes from the Persian Gulf' and help other Gulf states resist 'outside threats of subversion'.[7]

In the shah, Washington found a ready collaborator. For under the Nixon Doctrine, Iran would play a role that accorded perfectly with the shah's own vision of Iran's rightful place as the predominant regional power. He regarded the Persian Gulf as his country's 'jugular vein' and vowed to ensure the flow of trade through the Strait of Hormuz, Shatt al-Arab, and the Gulf waterways as a whole. When the British announced their decision to withdraw from the Gulf by the end of 1971, the shah resolved to fill the void, protecting conservative states against radical insurgency, counteracting Soviet efforts to gain increased influence, acting as a stabilising force in a region undergoing rapid socioeconomic change. Indeed, the shah was so eager to assume paramountcy in the Gulf that he proclaimed in 1969, that *all* great powers should stay out of the Indian Ocean – the United States included.[8]

Nor did the shah's vision stop with the Persian Gulf. In his 1972 Navy Day address on Kharg Island, he confessed that until three or four years before, he had only thought of defending the Persian Gulf. But now he had more expansive ideas:

> Most of our wealth was obtained from Bandar Abbas and from the Hormuz Strait at that time, so we only wanted to preserve this wealth and to maintain free access to the outside world. But events were such that we were soon compelled to think of the Oman Sea and Iran's shores on the Oman Sea as well. And again world events were such that we were compelled to accept the fact that the sea adjoining the Oman Sea – I mean the Indian Ocean – does not recognise borders.
>
> And now, as far as our thoughts are concerned, we are no longer thinking only about guarding Abadan or Khorramshahr or Bushire or even Bandar Abbas or Hormuz. We are not even thinking only of guarding Jask and Chah Bahar. As for Iran's security limits – I will not state how many kilometres we have in mind, but anyone who is acquainted with geography and the strategic situation, and especially with the potential air and sea forces, knows what distances from Chah Bahar this limit can reach.[9]

From the early 1970s until his fall from power in January 1979, the shah took mighty strides to realise his dreams. His diplomacy moved from success to success. He understood the contradiction between his effort to forge a conservative, monarchical consensus in the Gulf and the fears that his hegemonic ambitions would provoke among the traditionalist states he purported to defend. During 1968 and 1969, he negotiated agreements with Saudi Arabia, Kuwait and Qatar to divide the continental shelf of the Persian Gulf. In January 1969 he effectively abandoned a longstanding Iranian claim on Bahrain – renouncing any use of force to settle the issue. The Majlis then endorsed a subsequent UN Security Council resolution (passed in 1970) affirming the view that the majority of the Bahrain populace desired full independence and sovereignty. In addition, he sought to improve relations with the three most powerful non-traditional Arab states. His ties with the Sadat regime in Egypt became increasingly warm and supportive during the 1970s: Sadat, in his moderate, pro-Western persona, was a natural partner in the conservative front that the shah hoped to build against radicalism and Soviet expansion. By forging a Tehran–Cairo axis, the shah forced hostile regimes in Syria and Iraq to come to terms. In 1972, Tehran and Damascus agreed to an exchange of ambassadors and concluded an economic agreement involving Iranian credits for Syria. In 1975, the Iraqis, now faced with isolation, settled the Iran–Iraq dispute over control of the Shatt al-Arab waterway, receiving as a quid pro quo Iran's promise to eliminate support and sanctuary for Kurdish separatists fighting in northern Iraq.[10]

This diplomatic activity, impressive though it was, only supplemented the shah's military designs. To place the Persian Gulf and Indian Ocean area under the shah's 'protection' required a massive upgrading of Iran's military power. In 1970, the shah commenced a huge armament programme through which he equipped the Iranian army, navy and air force with some of the most sophisticated products of modern weapons technology. He concluded agreements for the purchase of a large fleet of hovercraft (to facilitate rapid deployment of Iranian forces to Persian Gulf trouble spots), Spuance-class destroyers (the most advanced US design), French missile-firing patrol boats, Harpoon missiles, German and American submarines, attack and utility helicopters, British Chieftain tanks, F–4, F–5, and F–16 fighter aircraft, an array of anti-tank and anti-aircraft devices, and even Soviet SAM–7 and SAM–9 missiles.[11]

The shah's armed forces were not just for show. He gave clear, early evidence of his willingness to employ them. In 1971, shortly before Britain's departure from the Persian Gulf, the shah seized the strategic islands of the two Tumbs and Abu Musa, located at the mouth of the Strait of Hormuz. He garrisoned the former territory by agreement with the Arab sheikdom of Sharjah, but he could not reach a similar understanding with Ras al-Khaimah on the Tumbs. The shah occupied the islands by force. When the Arab police on Greater Tumb resisted, there were four fatalities, three of them Iranian.

By occupying these strategic points, the shah laid the groundwork for pursuing future naval ambitions in the northwest quadrant of the Indian Ocean. His immediate aim, however, was to prevent the islands from falling under the influence of revolutionary nationalist forces represented by the Popular Front for the Liberation of the Arabian Gulf (PFLOAG). In early 1972, the shah committed Iranian forces to antisubversive war against this group in Oman. Following initial PFLOAG guerrilla successes in Dhofar province during 1971, the Shah sent 2000 to 3000 lavishly equipped counterinsurgency troops, backed by airpower and heavy artillery, into Oman, where they played a prime role in breaking the rebellion. In 1977, the shah declared that any Persian Gulf state could avail itself of such assistance. He indeed extended aid beyond the Gulf area; helicopters and logistic support were provided to Pakistan in 1973–5 in order to crush an uprising by the Baluchi Popular Front. Later, in 1978, he began shipping weapons to Somalia to strengthen the Siad Barre government in its struggle against Soviet backed Ethiopia.[12]

The shah's drive for regional paramountcy was fuelled by American arms. Throughout the entire period of Fiscal Year 1950 to Fiscal Year 1970, Iranian–US military sales agreements totalled $790.525 million. In Fiscal Year 1971, American foreign military sales (FMS) agreements with Iran were in the sum of $354.613 million, rising to $455.615 million during the next year. In Fiscal Years 1973 and 1974, FMS agreements rose steeply (to $2133.680 million and $3950.069 million respectively) in the aftermath of the revenue windfall resulting from the huge oil price increases of 1973–4.[13] It should be noted, however, that Iranian military purchases were already on the way up before the quantum leap in oil prices. By 1971, the shah had already agreed on the purchase of the F–4 Phantom jets, British tanks, missile frigates and hovercraft, and transport and general use helicopters. He had built, or was building, new naval or air bases at Bandar Abbas, Jask, Bushire and Kurramshar. In May 1972, President Nixon went to Tehran after the Moscow summit encounter with Brezhnev. While there, he gave the Shah permission to purchase any US non-nuclear weapons system of the ruler's fancy – including F–14 or F–15 aircraft which were then at issue. When Nixon returned to Washington, he ordered the bureaucracy not to second-guess any future Iranian orders. This policy was continued during the Gerald Ford administration, belying any notion that the US blank cheque was purely Nixon's idea. For as Kissinger explained in his memoirs, the Iranian armament drive accorded with US global strategy. Owing to the Vietnam trauma, the United States could not play a balancing role in the Indian Ocean and Persian Gulf. But by arming Iran, Washington would enable a regional power to do what America could not.[14]

The shah's strategic vision also accorded with US thinking. The State Department winked at his takeover of Abu Musa and the two Tumb Islands. The Iranian landings, the department declared, had to be viewed in the total context of the events in the Persian Gulf. Such developments, if taken in their entirety, were in the interests of all littoral states and represented 'an affirmative contribution to the peace and security of the region'.[15] The shah's desire to extend his power to a huge, undefined quadrant of the Indian Ocean met as well with Washington's approval. A 'balanced blue water navy' would enable him to protect the sea approaches to the Persian Gulf;[16] and an Iranian counterweight to India would check her designs on Pakistan.[17]

SAUDI ARABIA

The Saudi ruling family had none of the grandiose ambitions of the shah. Their country, sparsely populated and tempting in its oil wealth, was surrounded by enemies. It shared borders with Ba'athist Iraq and Marxist South Yemen. Somalia (until it expelled the Soviets in 1977) and Ethiopia (after 1974) were no friends of Riyadh. And as for monarchical Iran, the Saudis derived scant comfort from the shah's military might that could some day be used against them.

To modernise their military, the Saudis not only purchased American weapons, but also followed American plans. At the request of the Riyadh government, a series of Defense Department surveys were undertaken during the late 1960s and early 1970s to assess Saudi military needs. These surveys, adhered to closely by the Saudi government, resulted in US–Saudi agreements to modernise the Navy, Air Force and National Guard. The United States Army Corps of Engineers was already deeply involved in the building of Saudi military infrastructure, contracted for under the engineer assistance programme of 1965. This involvement would continue and expand.[18]

As in the case of Iran, the Saudi armament programme brought huge expenditures on American weaponry. US–Saudi FMS agreements jumped from $15.245 million in Fiscal Year 1971 to $305.426 million in Fiscal Year 1972, the last year before the oil price boom. Soaring oil prices carried FMS agreements to $1152.036 million, $2048.234 million and $5775.999 million in Fiscal Years 1973, 1974 and 1975.[19] Unlike Iran, however, the Saudis were not given carte blanche to purchase any systems they wanted. There was strong resistance in US defence circles to letting them purchase a state-of-the-art fighter on the order of the F–14, F–15 or F–16. But by the end of 1975 this barrier came down: Secretary of State Kissinger had convinced

President Ford to allow the sale of any advanced aircraft the Saudis desired, including the coveted F-15.[20]

Along with improvement in their military posture, the Saudis flexed financial and political muscle in the cause of conservative stability. Egypt, Jordan, Syria and the Yemen Arab Republic (YAR) received substantial subsidies to reward 'moderate' behaviour. A ten-year YAR military modernisation programme was planned jointly by Washington and Riyadh and financed with Saudi cash. The Saudis contributed money and military training missions to operations against the PFLOAG in Dhofar.[21] The Saudis also harassed their foes. Starting in 1969, they sought to overthrow the People's Democratic Republic of Yemen (PDRY) by backing dissident and exile elements, including foreign-led tribal mercenaries, and supporting the YAR in its recurrent border warfare with the Aden regime. Eritrean rebels fought Ethiopian troops with arms purchased by Riyadh. Later, when the Mogadishu government threw the Soviets out of Somalia, the Saudis gave Somalia weapons to pursue irredentist ambitions in the Ethiopian province of the Ogaden.[22]

THE NAVY RE-ENTERS THE INDIAN OCEAN

The twin pillars would not be left to stand alone. Nixon propped up Saigon with massive air support. He would prop up the twin pillars with US sea power. A US naval presence in the Indian Ocean would provide a continuing display of Washington's interest in the region, reminding potential adversaries that America was still around. It would also provide – in the form of carrier-based aircraft – a potent, and highly flexible, means of exerting power in support of allied nations. Nixon, by the logic of his doctrine, embraced a maritime strategy for Persian Gulf defence, although the logic took time to unfold.

In 1965, the US naval build-up off the coast of Vietnam had drained Navy resources, putting a quick stop to the regular Indian Ocean deployments ordered in 1964. As Nixon reduced the direct US combat role in Vietnam, ships gradually became available once more for Indian Ocean duty.[23] In late 1971 and early 1972, naval and defence spokesmen announced that the United States would resume naval activity in the Indian Ocean. They justified this move on the grounds of the Nixon Doctrine, with its stress on supporting overseas allies through sea and air power.[24]

Such statements, which seemed to herald a more active US role in the Indian Ocean and Persian Gulf areas, were premature. At the time, advocates of a low-profile approach had the upper hand. So long as conditions remained as stated in the 1969–70 policy reviews, they saw no need for a further, direct effort on the part of the United States. However, a vocal minority objected to this assessment. The minority view would prevail in the end.

The Navy was an obvious centre of dissent. It was burdened, along with all the services, by strong cost-cutting pressures from an administration intent on halting inflation. As the price for increasing its shipbuilding budget, the Navy was forced to retire large numbers of its older vessels. Over 100 ships were retired in Fiscal Year 1970 – more than 10 per cent of the Navy's active strength. Indian Ocean naval deployments provided a much-wanted rationale for maintaining force levels as Vietnamization proceeded, and for embarking on a vast shipbuilding programme (including a fourth nuclear carrier) delayed because of Vietnam.[25]

Not only in the Navy, but in the military establishment as a whole, dissenting officials challenged the strategic assumptions of the low-profile strategy. With significant State Department and NSC support, they argued that investments, oil and other important primary products made the Indian Ocean not a peripheral but a prime area of concern. Increasing Soviet political and military activity, occurring as it did in a context of local instability, dictated, in Admiral Zumwalt's words, 'a continuous and regular U.S. naval presence in the Indian Ocean, if possible in coordination with operations by the British, Australians, and whatever other allies, . . . upgrading the Middle East Force [and] . . . improving naval and air facilities on the island of Diego Garcia'.

President Nixon never decided between the competing strategies. Proponents of the low profile remained in the majority until the 1973 Arab–Israeli war. In any case, their strategy won by default: economic considerations, plus the absorption of US ships off Vietnam, made it impossible to operate vessels in the Indian Ocean. Moreover, until October 1973, proponents of a forward posture had a hard time proving any need to change course: up to then conditions seemed quite favourable in the Indian Ocean and Persian Gulf.[26]

But on 6 October 1973 war broke out in the Middle East. Frustrated by their failure to regain territories lost in the 1967 war, Egypt and Syria launched a co-ordinated assault against Israeli forces along the Suez Canal and on the Golan Heights. On 17 October the Organisa-

tion of Arab Petroleum Exporting Countries agreed on joint production and export cutbacks, including a complete embargo on exports to
the United States. On 5 November further cutbacks were announced.
World oil markets were thrown in chaos as prices soared. The Arabs
had given Washington an unpleasant taste of the 'oil weapon'.

The 1973 war resolved the strategic debate. The oil embargo
demonstrated America's direct, as opposed to indirect, vulnerability
to oil stoppages. This made military guarantees for vital oil shipments
look more important than before. Strategically, the Indian Ocean was
raised from tertiary to primary rank.[27]

On 28 October, three days after the final cease-fire, the attack
carrier *Hancock*, along with four other escorts and support auxiliaries,
was ordered into the Indian Ocean. The United States maintained
substantial naval forces there until April 1974. On 30 November 1973,
Defense Secretary Schlesinger announced resumption of the regular,
intermittent naval deployments in the Indian Ocean that had been
planned during the Johnson administration but were disrupted by
Vietnam. As the pattern developed, the augmented US presence
comprised three naval task group deployments per year, every other
one including an aircraft carrier.[28]

THE DEBATE OVER DIEGO GARCIA

The reintroduction of US naval forces to the Indian Ocean sparked
renewed interest in base support. Diego Garcia became once more a
focus of hot debate, though the arena shifted from the bureaucracy to
the Congress, where the Vietnam experience had provoked a renewed
Congressional assertiveness in defence policy and foreign affairs.

On 1 February 1974, the State Department sent a letter to members
of Congress informing them of the administration's plans to upgrade
the communications facility on Diego Garcia. To this end, a $29
million request was included in the Fiscal Year 1974 Supplemental
Military Appropriations Budget. The runway would be lengthened to
12 000 feet; a fuel storage depot built; the aircraft parking area
expanded; and the lagoon dredged out to provide better anchorage for
carrier task forces. Owing to stubborn Senate opposition, monies were
not forthcoming until November 1975, when Congress appropriated
$13.8 million as a first instalment. In the spring of 1976, the Diego
Garcia expansion at last began.[29]

In pushing Diego Garcia through a reluctant legislature, administration officials gave a less than full account of the context of the base expansion. From 1971 until 1973, they had disclaimed plans for regular Indian Ocean deployments or to build up Diego Garcia. To explain the apparent turnaround, they invoked recent events. The 1973 Middle East War, the energy crisis, the probable opening of the Suez Canal within two years (which would make it easier for Soviet ships to get into the Indian Ocean), and a growing Soviet naval presence in the Indian Ocean – all combined to underscore the need for increased US capabilities in the area and for a base to support them. It was these 'changing circumstances', in the words of Defense Secretary James Schlesinger, that pointed up the need for an ability 'to operate routinely on a sustained basis in the Indian Ocean and its environs'. But before the war, officials claimed, no plans existed for either increased naval operations or expanded facilities on Diego Garcia.[30]

By making so categorical a claim, administration policy makers were stating just part of the truth. Plans *did* exist, sitting on the shelf, waiting to be picked up and implemented. 'The fact that they had not been picked up was due more to constrained resources (and favourable circumstances) than to strategic design. By the logic of Nixon's strategy, however, the Navy had always been right.

US INTERESTS, THE SOVIET UNION AND THIRD WORLD CHANGE

The Navy had also been right by the logic of perceived US interests. In early 1974, 7.9 per cent of American oil came from the Persian Gulf. While the figure was not large, the oil embargo had demonstrated how even marginal supply disruptions could disorganise US petroleum markets. But this was not the most important consideration. US prosperity was linked to the fate of its major trading partners and allies. In 1974, approximately 80 per cent of Japan's and 64 per cent of Europe's oil supply came from the Middle East. Three years earlier, Robert Pranger, Deputy Assistant Secretary of Defense for International Security Affairs, noted the dangers of this dependence:

Interdiction of the flow of Persian Gulf oil to Japan and Western Europe could cripple those economies in a very short period of time. Alternate supplies to meet the vast fuel requirements of these industrial nations would not be readily available, and in any event, major realignment of supply sources and distribution systems would be required to keep these economies going without Persian Gulf oil.[31]

US interests had expanded, moreover, since Eisenhower's time. His Eurocentrism no longer defined the extent of US concern. Nixon policy makers saw the issue as one of defending not only Europe, but an entire world economy that had grown increasingly interlinked. The United States would have to protect this interest against the great power threat of the Soviet Union and regional threats of disorder and violent change.

As before, the first threat fed on the second. The Soviet Union's naval presence and military assistance programme had helped it expand its influence, but, in Pranger's words, had 'not themselves been the initiator of that influence'. Rather, the Soviets had enhanced their position by 'exploiting targets of opportunity among revolutionary and nationalist forces in the region'. They were aided in this by historical circumstance. Middle Eastern nationalism had been forged in struggle against Western domination. It took on, therefore, 'an anti-Western hue'. Popular yearnings for modernisation and reform, to the degree that they assumed an anti-capitalist bias, also served Soviet ends.[32]

Yet, even if the Soviets were not a factor, the United States would still need to safeguard its interests against endemic instability in the region. This, policy makers said, was one of the reasons for building up the Diego Garcia base. In Admiral Zumwalt's view, while Soviet naval activity *added* 'to the rationale for Diego Garcia, that rationale would exist independently of anything the Soviets are doing.'[33] Noting that the US presence 'predated any concern with the Soviet Union', Seymour Weiss, Director of the State Department Bureau of Politico–Military Affairs, asserted, 'we would retain capability in that area whether or not there were Soviet forces.'[34] 'We have,' he said, 'a range of interests which stem from the sheer instability of the area.' Diego Garcia 'related to an entire spectrum of . . . considerations, only one of which bears on the level of Soviet deployments' in the Indian Ocean.[35] Conservative governments were threatened by anti-Western radical groups like the PFLOAG in Oman. Soviet-armed Iraq threatened Saudi Arabia and Kuwait. War could erupt between India (signatory to a 1971 Indo–Soviet friendship treaty) and Pakistan, Ethiopia and Somalia, and the PDRY and YAR. Small bands of terrorists, armed with modern weapons, could sabotage shipping through the Strait of Hormuz. In such cases, the United States might have to step in to assert its interests and protect its allies. Because of the distance of the Persian Gulf from any land-based centre of US power, an intervention would have to employ naval forces, which would enter the area using the Indian Ocean as the avenue of approach.

PLUS ÇA CHANGE, PLUS ÇA RESTE. . .

It would be a mistake to view the post-1973 events as a watershed in US policy, as many observers have done. Stepped-up naval deployments and the Diego Garcia expansion were products of a strategy and world view that pre-dated 1973. The United States had set on a course of opposing change. It did so not only in the Middle East, but also in Southern Africa, where it 'tilted' toward the white supremist regimes in Southern Rhodesia and South Africa, and supported Portuguese colonialism in Angola and Mozambique. The low profile strategy was conditioned not on acceptance of change, but on the ability of surrogates to suppress it. If US forces were spared the job then so much the better. But as soon as the underlying assumptions of the low-profile strategy changed, it was simple logic to commit US forces to the task, not to supplant reliance on regional actors, but to stiffen their confidence and power.

The policy was rife with contradiction. Officials recognised that the instabilities of the region were rooted in historical and social developments it would be difficult to control through military force. But they sought military solutions nonetheless. The events of 1973 imparted a comic quality to their quest. The entire 7th Fleet could not have kept the oil flowing against the decision of Arab producers to cut it off. America's Saudi surrogate embargoed oil along with radical Iraq; and Nixon's good friend, the shah, led OPEC hawks who wanted to keep oil prices high and rising. Washington's response to the economic damage its friends had done was to commit itself more deeply to protecting these 'friends' from radical, terrorist or Soviet enemies.

Equally anomalous was Washington's failure to draw the most obvious lesson from the war. The Arab oil embargo had given decisive lie to the notion that the Persian Gulf was a distinct strategic theatre, separable from the rest of the Middle East. For the embargo was not triggered by events in the Persian Gulf *per se*: rather, it was triggered by the war – another violent manifestation of the Arab struggle with Israel.

Yet the implication of this eluded policy makers. The strengthening of Naval capabilities in the Indian Ocean, and of the Saudi and Iranian armed forces, were at a far remove from dealing with the core issue of the Arab–Israeli conflict.

To be sure, for eight months after the war, Secretary of State Kissinger took a direct hand in brokering Egyptian–Israeli and Syrian–Israeli disengagement accords: his 'step-by-step' diplomacy. These accords, however, in no way aimed for a comprehensive peace. They were designed to stabilise the situation vis-à-vis Israel and the Arab 'frontline' governments while isolating the Palestinians.

WASHINGTON DENIES PALESTINIAN NATIONALISM

Indeed, the Palestinians became one of the prime targets of Nixon's repressive project in the Middle East. For Nixon policy makers considered Palestinian nationalism as a hostile, illegitimate force, unworthy of recognition. US officials did not hide the fact that they would have preferred to treat the Palestinians as mere refugees, lacking national identity and national claims. Writing in his memoirs, Kissinger noted that prior to 1973 the Palestinians did not appear as a major issue in international negotiations: the 1972 communiqué ending Nixon's Moscow summit meeting made no reference to the Palestinians; the abortive 'general working principles', discussed between Gromyko and Kissinger in 1972 mentioned them only as refugees; and although the 1973 US–Soviet summit communiqué spoke of 'legitimate' Palestinian interests, these were not defined.[36]

Kissinger's concept of the Palestinian issue as one of refugees, instead of an emerging nationalism, was outdated well before 1973. Palestinian resistance organisations had taken root by the early 1960s. The Arab Nationalist Movement, which identified with Nasser and espoused Arab unity as a means to win back Palestine, had become a centralised political party in the mid-1950s. The Fatah organisation was formally constituted in 1959, and launched its first military operation against Israel in early 1965. In January 1964 delegates to the first Arab summit meeting in Cairo approved the establishment of a Palestine Liberation Organisation (PLO) and a Palestine Liberation Army (PLA). The PLO was constituted four months later under pro-Egyptian leadership.

The 1967 Six-Day War gave a powerful boost to the Palestinian national movement. The humiliating Arab defeat proved the weakness of Arab governments and the hollowness of pan-Arab rhetoric. The idea that the Palestinians could only count on themselves gained increasing currency. The pro-Egyptian leaders of the PLO were forced out; and by 1968 the organisation had been reformed, under Fatah's aegis, into an umbrella organisation encompassing a range of resistance groups of various ideological persuasions. This merger was formalised on 17 July 1968 with the adoption of a Palestine National Covenant.

For Kissinger, the PLO presented itself 'largely as a terrorist group'. PLO participation in peace negotiation would be 'disruptive'.[37] There would be no use for PLO involvement in any event, because the United States could not accept even the minimalist PLO demand for a 'mini-state' on the West Bank and Gaza Strip. Such a state, Kissinger explained, would be surely 'irredentist'.[38] Extremist factions would prevent it from changing its professed aims; and its Soviet ties would draw it toward the radicalism of states like Libya or South Yemen. Moreover, PLO hints at possible coexistence with Israel could not be believed. In Kissinger's eyes, the most moderate PLO policy euphemistically called for a Moslem–Jewish–Christian secular state that meant the dismantlement of Israel. Even should Israel withdraw to its 1967 borders and surrender the old city of Jerusalem, the Palestinians would covet the whole of former Palestine: a West Bank mini-state 'could be only an intermediate step toward their final aims'.[39] Kissinger never bothered explaining how he came to such conclusions prior to any effort to explore avenues of accommodation with the PLO. His diplomacy was aimed rather at assuring that the exploration never occurred. Insofar as the Palestinian problem figured in peace talks, Kissinger declared, it should be as part of negotiations between Jordan and Israel. That, as he stated on 15 July, would provide the 'most efficient means for the Palestinians to be brought into the process'.[40]

In pushing for a negotiation between Jordan and Israel, Kissinger dismissed a resolution, passed by the conference of Arab heads of government, assembled in Algiers on 26–8 November 1973, recognising the PLO as the sole representative of the Palestinians. While the resolution was not unanimous, owing to a Libyan, Iraqi and Jordanian boycott of the conference, unanimity later prevailed at the Rabat summit of October 1974.

Yet, despite the Arab consensus recognising the PLO, Washington still espoused the 'Jordanian option', even after Rabat.[41] If the United States were to deal with the PLO, Kissinger stipulated, the Palestinians would have to accept Israel's right to exist and abide by UN

Security Council Resolutions 242 and 338. Until the PLO fulfilled these requirements, the United States would never recommend that Israel negotiate with it, 'because we cannot encourage a negotiating process between parties one of which wants to destroy the other and has as its avowed policy to destroy the other'.[42]

Kissinger's demands on the PLO were advanced not as conditions leading to Palestinian involvement in Middle East peace discussions, but as window dressing for his policy of blocking the PLO out. The PLO could not recognise Israel when Israel adamantly refused, under any circumstances, to deal with the PLO. Resolution 242 mentioned the Palestinians only as a 'refugee problem', thus denying their national claims, and Resolution 338 failed to mention them at all. Kissinger did not make any countervailing demands on Israel; and in his eagerness to confer international legitimacy on his policy by invoking Security Council Resolutions 242 and 338, he neglected General Assembly Resolution 3236 – passed on 22 November 1974 – which affirmed Palestinian rights to self-determination and to national independence and sovereignty.[43]

In the meantime, Washington bolstered its status quo diplomacy with massive arms shipments to Israel – foreign military sales deliveries of $3.4 billion for Fiscal Years 1974–7.[44] Israel became a regional superpower, under no pressure, and without compunction, to compromise on the Palestinians and the occupied West Bank – especially in view of American hostility toward the PLO. Thus, a great point of tension would remain. Policy makers who saw security as a function of military power in the Indian Ocean and Persian Gulf would not be overly concerned with relieving it.

5 Carter Closes the Clasp

Few administrations produced such sharp divergences between promise and performance as the administration of Jimmy Carter. And in no area of policy was the divergence so great as in the Middle East.

To some extent, Carter's experience paralleled John F. Kennedy's. Kennedy entered office with the promise of reconciling America with Third World nationalism. He pursued detente with Nasser and sought a political settlement to the Palestinian problem. But he ended by embracing the status quo and laying the groundwork for a strategy of military repression. Likewise, in his first year as president, Carter played down East–West conflict in order to strengthen US ties with the Third World. He pressed for a comprehensive peace in the Middle East and for PLO involvement in negotiations. By the end of his term, however, he had brokered an Egyptian–Israeli separate peace which gave *carte blanche* to an ultra-right Israeli government intent on crushing Palestinian nationalism by brute force, and had unabashedly militarised US policy toward the region, ordering a massive build-up of American military capabilities in the Indian Ocean and Persian Gulf.

EARLY CARTER AND THE COMPREHENSIVE PEACE

Much of the inconsistency that surrounds Carter's foreign policy is attributable to factional divisions within his administration. On the one side were Carter 'hawks' (e.g., National Security Advisor Zbigniew Brzezinski, Defense Secretary Harold Brown, Brzezinski's aides Samuel Huntington and David Aaron), and on the other side, Carter 'doves' (e.g., Secretary of State Cyrus Vance, UN Ambassador Andrew Young, Arms Control and Disarmament Director Paul Warnke). The first group viewed Third World events through the prism of East–West global conflict and defined US security in terms of maintaining the politico-military status quo. The second group were concerned that 'U.S./Soviet issues [should] not be permitted to so dominate our foreign policy that we neglect other important relationships and problems.' They looked forward to bringing 'a new sensitivity, awareness and priority to the . . . relationship between industrialized and the unindustrialized world, and the new . . . issues that are emerging, such as energy, population, environment and nuclear proliferation'.[1]

Yet, with respect to the early administration position on the Middle East there was uncommon consensus. Both Vance and Brzezinski agreed that the 'step-by-step approach had exhausted its potential and it was time to renew the pursuit of a comprehensive peace'.[2] There were no more 'small steps' to take; and without resolution of the difficult issues of the Palestinians and the occupied Arab territories, 'the stalemate that existed in 1977 would gradually fragment, with disastrous consequences for world peace as well as for the United States itself'.[3] In particular, the Palestinians could not be ignored. They presented, in Vance's view, 'the central, unresolved, human rights issue in the Middle East'. No lasting settlement would be possible unless 'a just answer to the Palestinian question could be found, one almost certainly leading to a Palestinian homeland and some form of self-determination'.[4] Brzezinski concurred, his own ideas having been influenced by participation in a 1975 Brookings Institution panel on the Middle East, which issued a report advocating 'Palestinian self-determination' that 'might take the form of an independent Palestinian state . . . or of a Palestinian entity voluntarily federated with Jordan but exercising an extensive political autonomy'.[5] This report was endorsed by presidential candidate Jimmy Carter.

Unlike previous administrations which proposed to dispose of the Palestinians *qua* 'refugees', who would have no say in their fate, Carter officials recognised, in the words of a State Department release of 12 September 1977, that 'to be lasting, a peace agreement must be positively supported by all the parties to the conflict, including the Palestinians'.[6] They understood, moreover, that genuine Palestinian participation meant participation by the PLO. (Any notion that a non-PLO 'silent majority' of West Bank 'moderates' represented the majority of Palestinians was erased with the shattering victory of avowed PLO supporters in the 1976 West Bank municipal elections, held under Israeli auspices.) The major issue for US policy was not, then, the principle of PLO participation, but the formula by which to bring it about. (Washington preferred including PLO representatives in a unified Arab delegation.)

As a forum for achieving a comprehensive settlement, administration planners chose a reconvened Geneva Middle East Peace Conference, which had been lying dormant after its first meeting in December 1973. For the better part of 1977, Carter negotiators strove to bring the contending parties (including the PLO) to Geneva. Washington enlisted the involvement of the Soviet Union, in its capacity as co-chairman (along with the United States) of the conference. The efforts culminated in a US–USSR joint communiqué of 1 October 1977 declaring the commitment of both governments to a fundamental solution to the Middle East conflict, 'incorporating all parties concerned and all questions'. [7]

On 9 November, however, Egyptian President Anwar Sadat snatched the initiative from Washington with a dramatic announcement that he would go to Jerusalem and talk peace with the Israelis. Ten days later he made his journey, and on 20 November addressed the Knesset.

The administration quickly embraced the Sadat *démarche*. Nevertheless, it was well aware that Egyptian–Israeli negotiations could jeopardise chances for a wider peace: the fact that Sadat had not consulted other Arab leaders could leave him 'isolated and exposed',[8] and if talks led only to an Egyptian–Israeli separate peace, the result 'would be inherently unstable'.[9] Accordingly, Vance wanted the United States to use the discussions as a stepping stone to Geneva. Brzezinski spoke of a 'concentric circles approach' – building on the Egyptian–Israeli accord, then expanding the circles to include Jordan and West Bank and Gaza Strip Palestinians, and then, at the end of the process, engaging the Syrians and perhaps the Soviets in a comprehensive settlement.[10]

In early 1978 it became increasingly clear that the Geneva conference would not materialise, nor would the concentric circles ever expand. As Sadat's initiative reached stalemate, despite a presidential trip to the Middle East in January, Carter began to lean toward sponsorship of an Egyptian–Israeli peace, which might be easier to attain if separated from other, more intractable, issues. To veil his retreat from a goal of a comprehensive settlement, and in an effort to make the proposition minimally tolerable to other Arab states, he would try to link this peace to some sort of 'progress' on the West Bank.[11]

Carter was edging steadily back to the very step-by-step diplomacy he had rejected only a year before. The Camp David 'peace framework' marks the culmination of this process of retreat.

After Sadat's trip to Jerusalem initial hopes were dampened as subsequent talks reached stalemate. Carter broke the stalemate by bringing Sadat and Israeli Prime Minister Menachem Begin together for a conference at Camp David on 2–17 September 1978. This conference, too, seemed headed toward deadlock as both Egypt and the United States tried to push for Israeli concessions on the question of West Bank and Gaza Strip autonomy. The best Israel would offer was limited self-government in the context of continued Israeli rule, while Egypt pressed for the right of Palestinians to decide their own future after a five-year transitional period. The Israelis flatly rejected a US demand for a freeze on West Bank Jewish settlements during the course of negotiations.

Early in the second week of the conference, however, Carter devised a way out of the impasse. In a meeting with his staff, he expressed concern that in their preoccupation with the West Bank and the Gaza Strip – 'the core of the framework of the comprehensive settlement' – US negotiators had overlooked chances for an Egyptian–Israeli peace treaty. 'He noted that not only the differences on the Egyptian–Israeli bilateral issues seemed less profound in this area, but also that the presence of Sadat and Begin provided a unique opportunity to negotiate a framework for a peace treaty between two of our closest and most dependable friends in the Middle East.'[12]

The upshot of Carter's headlong dash to the rear was the two part Camp David 'peace framework'. One part provided for an Egyptian–Israeli peace treaty that would return the Sinai to Egypt in return for full diplomatic, cultural and trade relations and strict limitation on Egyptian forces there. The other part of the framework provided for multilateral negotiations (between Egypt, Israel, Jordan and 'representatives of the Palestinian people') on an autonomy arrangement for Arab residents of the West Bank and the Gaza Strip. The treaty between Egypt and Israel was signed with great fanfare in a ceremony on the White House lawn on 26 March 1978 – 'a glorious event', said Carter.[13]

But the glorious event of an Egyptian–Israeli separate peace was not followed by movement on the autonomy talks. Nor was such movement likely. As Brzezinski admitted, the link between the Egyptian–Israeli peace and the West Bank–Gaza Strip negotiations was 'vague' – something of a 'fig leaf for Sadat'.[14] US negotiators thought they had obtained Israeli agreement to halt further West Bank settlements pending the completion of the autonomy talks, but when the Israelis delivered a side letter to confirm the understanding (on the promise of which the United States agreed to delete a settlement moratorium clause from the proposed accord), the letter mentioned only a moratorium during the three-month period of negotiations for an Egyptian–Israeli peace.[15] But since the side letter came one day after Carter, Sadat and Begin had signed the accords, nothing could be done.

The Israeli trick on Carter boded ill for subsequent autonomy discussions. Yet in a sense, Carter was willing to be tricked. His own interest in the Palestinians had flagged. As early as December 1977 he had begun to wash his hands of them. In an informal talk with reporters on 25 December 1977 he stated, 'I've never favored a separate nation or independent state of the Palestinians.' He followed this with a tepid utterance that 'anything that Prime Minister Begin would work out with the Jordanians or the Palestinians or the Egyptians would suit us.' On his trip to the Middle East in January 1978 he aired the notion of giving Palestinians a dictated choice of international administration or a federation with Jordan, yet quickly softened even this proposal by saying that he would not object if a different settlement were worked out by the other parties.[16] Now, after the signing of the Egyptian–Israeli peace, Carter made clear to his subordinates that he would no longer play a visible role in the Middle East. The autonomy negotiations would be handled by a special negotiator who would act as Carter's 'political shield'. (The position was held first by Robert Strauss, and then by Sol Linowitz.) Carter also wanted to avoid being bothered with the problem of Israeli settlements on the West Bank – meaning that no US pressure would be exerted to keep Israel from resolving the issue by de facto annexation. Without top level US participation in the talks, and with no American effort to stop Israeli annexationism, they were doomed from the outset. They were suspended on 4 December 1980 with no agreement on any significant political or economic issues.[17]

The administration had abandoned the goal of a comprehensive peace that it had earlier deemed essential to enduring stability in the Middle East. This abandonment was due partially to the power of the pro-Israel lobby in the United States, and partially to the feeling, which grew stronger in the wake of revolutionary disturbances in Iran, that an Egyptian–Israeli peace would constitute a strategic asset for the United States, even if other issues remained unresolved.

Yet, what the Carter retreat illustrates most of all is the chasm separating official articulation of a problem and effective action to achieve solutions. To accomplish the latter requires the conviction that a goal is vital enough to justify the cost of attaining it. The fact that a comprehensive peace was seen as greatly *desirable*, and perhaps necessary *in the long run*, did not make it sufficiently *vital* for Carter to incur the political costs of a showdown with Israel. Policy makers may have spoken of the 'need' to achieve an all-round settlement in order to preserve general stability in the area, but the linkage between an Arab–Israeli settlement (which demanded recognition of Palestinian nationalism and participation by the PLO) was not really so close in the minds of some officials as their rhetoric would suggest. In their final reckoning, US fundamental interests resided in the Persian Gulf – and would be defended in the Gulf *per se*. Moreover, the Gulf was still to them – as for Nixon–Ford policy makers – a separate theatre (part of the Indian Ocean) from the rest of the Middle East. Indeed, US policy toward the Indian Ocean and Persian Gulf had proceeded largely on lines of its own, following the logic not of Carter's purported commitment to a just and enduring peace for the region, but of Nixon's programme for repressive 'stability'.

CARTER WARMS OVER THE NIXON DOCTRINE

The first years of the Carter presidency brought few substantial changes in the Persian Gulf policies of Nixon and Ford. The twin pillar strategy was reaffirmed, particularly in respect to Iran. Indeed, despite Carter's early advocacy of human rights, he trumpeted effusive praises of the shah, proclaiming, 'Our military alliance is unshakeable, and it's an alliance that is beneficent in its impact on the rest of the world.' While arms transfers were subject to more restrictions, ending the 'blank cheque' treatment of Iran, US weapons agreements with non-Iranian allies continued to swell. Moreover, the diminution of sales to Iran reflected, in part, the effects of an oil price freeze between October 1975 and January 1977 (which forced the shah to economise on future arms purchases), and, in part, the belief that since the shah had already been armed to the hilt with the best American equipment, further, unbridled diffusion of advanced military technology was neither prudent nor necessary. In any case, throughout the Middle East as a whole (subtracting Iran), the Carter administration stepped up, rather than slowed down, US weapons reinforcements of America's allies. 1978 witnessed exceptionally large boosts in arms sales agreements with Saudi Arabia and Israel, and also marked the beginning of an increasingly close security relationship between the United States and Anwar Sadat's Egypt. [18]

The direct US military presence in the region remained unchanged. Work proceeded on the Diego Garcia base. The practice of deploying three task forces a year to the Indian Ocean continued as before.

The only new démarche was the president's proposal, articulated in a press conference on 9 March 1977, to conclude a treaty with the Soviet Union demilitarising the Indian Ocean – and offer subsequently modified to comprise 'mutual military restraint'. The Soviets displayed interest; and between June 1977 and February 1978 Soviet and American negotiators met four times to discuss the issue. Considerable progress was made, including agreement on a basic formula by which each side would freeze the status quo, keeping forces and patterns of deployment as they were, with no new bases or expansion of existing facilities. But after the February session Washington suspended the talks. The immediate cause of the suspension was a large increase in Soviet naval activity, coupled with Cuban combat intervention, during the Somali–Ethiopian conflict over the Ogaden. A wider question, however, was in dispute: how to define great power 'rules of the game' regarding intervention in local or regional hostilities.

The talks would never resume – happily for Carter conservatives, who argued that a naval agreement could not restrain Soviet 'proxy' interventions (as by Cuba), nor could it reduce Soviet advantages of geography. Echoing the low profile advocates of the Nixon administration, arms control proponents had been more sanguine about US strength, pointing out that Washington would hold the upper hand in nearly all contingencies short of the one least likely to occur – an all-out Soviet invasion of Iran. In any case, notwithstanding conservative opposition, naval arms control was hardly a radical idea. For a freeze at prior force levels would have ensured US superiority. Not only were US naval task groups in the Indian Ocean vastly more powerful than Soviet naval forces, but the strategic balance as a whole was founded on regional surrogates the United States would continue to arm. Most of all, mutual great power naval restraint would not have diminished the military strength of Iran. A US–USSR naval arms accord would have served to complement the policy of putting primary reliance on the shah.[19]

By the end of 1978, however, the policy had collapsed in ruins. The rapid disintegration of the shah's regime, culminating in its inevitable downfall in early 1979, robbed Washington of its key strategic asset in the area. It would no longer be possible to rely so heavily on regional actors to safeguard the status quo. In order to compensate for the loss of the Iranian surrogate, US defence planners would commence feverish efforts to increase US strength in the region to a level that could not even be contemplated during the immediate post-Vietnam era. The centrepiece of these efforts would be the creation of a new Third World intervention capability – the Rapid Deployment Force (RDF).

AN ENCORE FOR THIRD WORLD INTERVENTION

The idea of creating a Third World intervention force (oriented toward the Persian Gulf) enjoyed its initial bureaucratic glimmering in the first summer of Carter's term. In July 1977, a five-month interagency overview of US force requirements was put before the president. This study, Presidential Review Memorandum 10 (PRM-10), provided a rationale for upgrading conventional US forces. In the strategic sphere, the study argued, the United States and Soviet Union were in a state of 'essential equivalence' that was not likely to change. Washington needed, however, to enhance its ability to defend against conventional attack in Europe, the Persian Gulf and the Far East.[20] One outcome of the report was Presidential Directive 18 (PD-18). Issued by Carter in August, it ordered – as part of an overall increase in US conventional capabilities – the establishment of a mobile 'quick reaction' force to fight limited wars in Third World milieus.

The quick reaction force appeared as a codicil in PD-18. Yet RDF advocates were quite serious in their intentions. For them, the international environment, particularly in Africa and the Middle East, was extremely unstable at the very time the United States was becoming increasingly dependent on it 'in trade, in raw materials, in energy and in a broad range of political relationships'.[21] This dependence resulted from the 'size and rapid expansion of the U.S. economy'. 'We are' asserted Secretary of Defense Harold Brown,

the world's principal international trader: on the one hand, we need international markets for our agricultural and high technology products; on the other hand, we depend increasingly on external sources of raw materials, with oil the most prominent and disturbing example of our dependence. For that reason alone, our interest and involvement in the Middle East and Persian Gulf are bound to be substantial, although our principal trading partners are in Canada, Japan and Western Europe.[22]

Explosive rivalries, terrorism and undeclared wars could at any time threaten these vital US interests. War could erupt among rival local forces with or without Soviet intervention. Such clashes, Brown declared, 'not only might require the dispatch of appropriate U.S. forces to the scene in support of friends; they could precede and even set off a crisis or a conflagration in Europe.'[23]

Despite such sentiments, shared by such important figures as Zbigniew Brzezinski and Samuel Huntington, the Rapid Deployment Force did not make headway until a year after PD-18. To begin with, there was no initial consensus in the administration for a hardline posture in the Indian Ocean and Persian Gulf areas. Brzezinski, Huntington and Brown represented what was for the time being a minority faction in an ideologically divided administration. Carter liberals were pushing a US–Soviet naval arms freeze in the Indian Ocean – and, as noted, they had the president's early support. Also, bureaucratic momentum was vitally lacking. Huntington tried to convince the Marine Corps that an intervention force would be in its institutional self-interest, but failed: the Marines were chiefly concerned with securing a good position for themselves in Europe.[24] Nor did the other services have any reason to press for implementation of PD-18. The RDF was not put into the budget. The Joint Chiefs bickered over command arrangements; action consisted mainly of doing paperwork exercises identifying extant forces the RDF might use.

But by August 1978 the anti-shah rumblings in Iran had grown to earthquake proportions. With the Iranian pillar tottering, Brzezinski became concerned over the lack of progress toward implementing PD-18: in September, he ordered planning accelerated. His concern was well-placed, for on 16 January 1979 the shah fled Iran. On 1 February the Ayatollah Khomeini staged his triumphal return – followed in short order by alarmed reports that the PDRY had invaded the YAR.

These reports were exaggerated – a point confirmed by first-hand observation of the supposed front by the US military attaché to the YAR, whose conclusions were corroborated by the Defense Intelligence Agency.[25] But the accuracy or inaccuracy of US intelligence was not the real issue. The situation was out of control. Not only had the shah's regime collapsed, but in April 1978 an avowedly Marxist regime had taken power in Afghanistan, followed in November by a Soviet–Ethiopian treaty. Along with these strategic setbacks came the assassination in Kabul of US Ambassador Dubs on 14 February 1979. The Carter administration felt hard pressed to show that it could exert influence in the region. The only way of doing so was through a display of military power.

In January 1979 Washington had already sent a squadron of F–15 fighters to Saudi Arabia on a five-day visit designed to bolster client state confidence in American resolve. In March, two American AWACS reconnaissance aircraft started operating out of Saudi territory to observe the fighting between North and South Yemen. US military equipment – part of a longstanding $390 million aid programme financed by the Saudis – began flowing to the YAR on a rush basis, accompanied by seventy US advisers. The aircraft carrier *Constellation* – boasting a complement of fifty fighters and attack aircraft – sailed from the Philipines along with a destroyer and cruiser escort.

This carrier deployment foreshadowed a strengthened US naval presence in the Indian Ocean. When the *Constellation* task force departed, in the middle of April, it was replaced by the carrier *Midway* – although the Yemen conflict had ceased in mid-March. Then, toward the beginning of July – and a little over a month after the *Midway* had left – another force, comprising a missile cruiser, three frigates and an oiler passed into the Indian Ocean through the Straits of Malacca. Thus, in five months the United States had deployed three task forces – equalling the prior level of activity for a full year.[26]

The increased deployments had been approved at a White House meeting of an NSC special coordinating committee in April. Another result of this meeting was a directive mandating interagency discussions to develop a broader 'security framework' for the Indian Ocean and Persian Gulf.[27] Under Brzezinski's prodding, planning for the framework proceeded over the spring and summer. One of the products was a major Pentagon study on US force requirements in the Persian Gulf – the so-called Wolfowitz Report, dated 15 June 1979. It concluded that the United States would need a variety of forces – marines, airborne forces, air cavalry, tactical air, or a naval 'presence' – to cope with potential involvements ranging from advisers and counterinsurgency specialists to a full-scale combat commitment. In a sentence italicised for emphasis it warned that since the existing contingency force was established for other purposes, it *'is not well suited to many of the problems it is likely to face'*.[28]

The framework had emerged in outline by 1 October, when President Carter, in two little-noticed passages embedded in his televised speech on a purported Soviet 'combat' brigade in Cuba, made his first public pronouncement on a policy which had been settled during the spring and summer months. 'The United States,' Carter declared,

> has a worldwide interest in peace and stability. Accordingly, I have directed the Secretary of Defense to further enhance the capacity of

our Rapid Deployment Forces to protect our own interests and to act in response to requests for help from our allies and friends. We must be able to move our ground, sea and air units to distant areas – rapidly and with adequate supplies.

Continuing, he noted, 'We have reinforced our naval presence in the Indian Ocean.'[29]

And so, the course was set – before the November seizure of the American Embassy in Tehran and the Soviet invasion of Afghanistan. These latter events gave added momentum to a process already in motion. By late October, the services received specific guidance on the command structure of the RDF. In the wake of the Iranian crisis, two carrier task forces were ordered into the Arabian Sea. A Pentagon team made its first visit to Kenya, Somalia and Oman shortly before Christmas to discuss military access to facilities in those countries. Earlier, in the summer, planning had begun further to expand the Diego Garcia base.[30] The Soviet invasion of Afghanistan on 26 December hastened, rather than initiated, the translation of plans and options into budgets and concrete realities.

This should come as no surprise. While Afghanistan brought an almost immediate increase in commitment of resources to Persian Gulf defence, it had no bearing either on US interests in the region, or on official perceptions of those interests. For it was not Soviet troops in Afghanistan but the very nature of the American and *world* economies that defined US objectives in the Indian Ocean and Persian Gulf. In the words of the Wolfowitz Report:

> The United States and its major industrial allies have a vital and growing stake in the physical security of the Persian Gulf region. This interest derives primarily, but not exclusively from the importance of Persian Gulf oil supplies. Although some industrial countries, e.g. Britain and Norway, may be able to diminish or eliminate their dependence upon this oil the interdependence of the Western economic system means that no country or group of countries could successfully insulate itself from the adverse economic and political effects that would occur if the Gulf oil flow were abruptly curtailed.[31]

CARTER THROWS DOWN THE GAUNTLET

In the month following the Soviet move into Afghanistan, the President launched a fierce rhetorical attack. Speaking on 4 January, Carter decried the invasion as 'a callous violation of international law and the United Nations' charter . . . [and] a deliberate effort of a powerful, atheistic government to subjugate an independent Islamic people'.[32] He struck his most strident chord in his State of the Union message of 23 January. 'The Soviet Union,' he declared, 'is going to have to answer some basic questions: Will it help promote a more stable international environment in which its own legitimate, peaceful concerns can be pursued or will it continue to expand its military power far beyond its genuine security needs, and use that power for colonial conquests?' After painting a grim picture of the Soviet threat to the free movement of Middle Eastern oil, Carter then asserted the 'Carter Doctrine': 'An attempt by any outside force to gain control of the Persian Gulf region will be regarded as an assault on the vital interests of the United States of America, and such an assault will be repelled by any means necessary including military force.'[33]

The last year of Carter's term was marked by feverish efforts to back the Carter Doctrine with military power. The RDF was put into the budget – a milestone in terms of translating ideas into substance – and the strategy for deploying it set out in detail. More striking yet was the dispatch with which the administration bolstered immediate US capabilities in the Indian Ocean region – an effort unparalleled in peacetime.

According to the administration's plan, unveiled in early 1980, a Rapid Deployment Joint Task Force (RDJTF) would be constituted as a subordinate element of the US Readiness Command at MacDill Airforce Base, Florida. No units would be assigned directly to the RDJTF. Rather, existing units that could be used for rapid deployment purposes would be put into a central reservoir which the RDJTF commander would tap as need arose. The forces originally placed in the reservoir numbered approximately 100 000, but later over 200 000 were identified for potential service in the RDF. When Third World crises occurred an appropriate force package would be assembled and put under operational command of the head of the RDJTF. Periodically, designated units would be placed under his command for training and exercise purposes.[34]

The two big problems for the RDF were the interrelated ones of mobility and logistics. To deal with them the administration proposed substantial increases in airlift and sealift capacities. The Navy would purchase or lease twelve to fifteen civilian-manned Maritime Prepositioning Ships (MPS) which would be stationed in potential trouble areas like the Indian Ocean. These ships would carry in dehumidified storage heavy equipment and supplies for three marine amphibious brigades (approximately 52 000 men, including a Marine airwing and Navy personnel). The Marines would move themselves and such equipment as was not suitable to this pre-positioning – in particular, helicopters and fixed wing aircraft – by air. They would rendezvous with pre-positioning vessels at or near the point of crisis and be ready for combat on short call. For the Army's needs a C-X programme was proposed to build a new fleet of cargo aircraft that could carry heavy outsized equipment over intercontinental distances and land in small, sparsely equipped airfields. Other airlift programmes already underway were: structural modification of C-5A wings (to prevent them from falling off) that would more than quadruple the life of the aircraft; a 'stretch' modification to increase the capacities of the C-141; and procurement of the KC-10 aerial tanker. Supplies would be moved to the Persian Gulf in bulk on eight high-speed SL7 container vessels. These ships, to be purchased from the Sea Land Corporation, could make 33 knots – 11.5 steaming days from the Persian Gulf. Together, they could carry an entire Army mechanised division.[35]

Facilities were also important. More money would be spent improving Diego Garcia. But while the island was originally seen as a substitute for continental bases, it would now be but a part – although a central one – in a much wider supply network in the region. 'Diego Garcia,' as the Under Secretary of Defense for Policy, Robert Komer, put it, 'can be viewed as the hub of the wheel with spokes extending to other areas on the Indian Ocean littoral.'[36] The United States would thus seek improved access to airfields and ports in Oman, increased US air and naval use of facilities at Mombasa, Embakasi and Nanyuki in Kenya, and use of air and port installations at Berbera and Mogadiscio in Somalia. Hundreds of millions would be spent to upgrade such facilities once agreement had been secured with the local governments.[37]

Most of these programmes would pay dividends only in the future. This would not satisfy the sharp desire felt in the administration to take immediate action. The quickest thing that could be done was to adopt a positive tone of policy, playing up what the United States could do in the here and now. In a 'not for attribution' briefing given in early February 1980, Komer described how Washington could put roughly 25 000 troops into the region in two weeks. The first element, a 1000-man Army battalion based in Italy, could be in the Gulf region in twenty-four hours armed with anti-tank weapons and mortars. A battalion from the 82nd airborne would arrive from the US a day later. A Marine airborne contingent of 1300 men could deploy in forty-eight hours; 2200 other Marines could come by sea within nine days. Within sixteen days, a full Marine brigade of 12 000 troops could arrive along with their equipment. An 8000-man heavy mechanised Army brigade replete with tanks and armoured personnel carriers could be airlifted from the United States in about the same time. Tactical air support could be provided from two aircraft carriers operating in the Indian Ocean; and one or two fighter squadrons could be moved into the region in thirty-six hours. 'So we can do something,' Komer said, 'we can do, even today, one hell of a lot more than some people seem to think. We can't do everything, but we'll be able to do more in a year and a lot more in two or three years. You've got to keep in mind that the Russians can't do everything, anymore than we can.'[38]

By the end of 1980 the administration could boast of considerable progress toward putting muscle into the Carter Doctrine. The RDJTF headquarters became operational on 1 March. Access agreements were signed with Oman (9 April), Kenya (22 June) and Somalia (22 August) for use of local facilities. Egypt gave an enthusiastic, though unwritten go-ahead for the transformation of both the Cairo West airport and the Ras Banas naval facilities on the Red Sea, directly across from central Saudi Arabia, into staging posts for the RDF. In February, a five-ship, 1800-man Marine Amphibious Unit, plus tanks, helicopters, artillery and anti-tank missiles, was ordered into the Arabian Sea. Such a force was scheduled for constant deployment, with units rotated from the Mediterranean and Pacific. Pending construction of the Maritime Pre-positioning Ships (the TAK-X programme), seven cargo and tanker ships were loaded with enough equipment, including fuel and water, to supply a 12 000-man Marine Amphibious Brigade, plus several Air Force squadrons, for two weeks. These interim cargo ships, known as the Nearterm Prepositioning Force (NTPF), had anchored at Diego Garcia by the end of July. The US naval presence in the Indian Ocean was maintained at roughly twenty-five ships, including two aircraft carriers with a complement of 150 airplanes. Air Force fighters and AWACs aircraft flew from Egyptian and Saudi Airfields to gain experience operating in the region. The Air Force also initiated B-52 reconnaissance flight into the Indian Ocean. When war erupted between Iran and Iraq in September 1980, Washington moved to forestall possible Iranian air strikes against Arab oil installations in the southern Persian Gulf: AWACs early warning aircraft were deployed to Saudi Arabia and a guided missile cruiser was sent into the Gulf to provide additional air defence capability. On 11 November the United States began airlifting 1400

troops, mainly from the 101st Airborne Division and the 150th Tactical
Fighter Group, to Egypt's Cairo West airport for ten days of desert
manoeuvres involving joint operations with their Egyptian counterparts. The unit from the 101st (a reinforced battalion) was transported
from Fort Campbell, Kentucky, with thirty-six helicopters, food, fuel,
ammunition, jeeps, trucks, anti-tank weapons, mortars, communications gear and light arms.[39]

Despite the stress on strengthening unilateral US intervention
capacities, Carter policy makers did not ignore US allies. As part of a
regional 'security framework' administration planners had hoped to
forge an informal alliance between Israel, Egypt, Saudi Arabia,
Jordan and the Persian Gulf monarchies. The hope was based,
however, on two vital assumptions: first, that the Saudis and the
Jordanians would acquiesce in the Egyptian–Israeli separate peace
signed in March 1979 (indeed, the Jordanians were expected to play a
direct role in the subsequent stages of the Camp David 'peace
process'); and second, that Arab fears of radicalism and the Soviet
Union would afford grounds for an implicit strategic relation with the
Israelis. Both assumptions proved illusory, despite personal efforts by
Brzezinski (author of the security framework concept) to bring
Amman and Riyadh in line.[40] But the Egyptians and Israelis were
showered with weapons largesse. President Sadat was particularly
eager to participate in the security framework, proposing that Egypt
assume the role of regional gendarme replacing the fallen shah. He
received $1.5 billion in military credits in connection with his peace
agreement with Israel. In early 1980 the administration announced the
decision to give him further credits of $1.1 billion over the next two
Fiscal Years and to permit him to buy F–15 and F–16 aircraft.[41] As
noted, Egyptian facilities at Ras Banas and Cairo West were put at
Washington's disposal. In mid-January 1980 a $400 million two-year
aid package was tendered to Pakistan. Although the Pakistanis
rejected it as insufficient, talks continued.[42] In the autumn, NSC, State
Department and Pentagon officials tried substantially to raise the ante
in Carter's last budget. They failed, but for fiscal, not strategic,
reasons; and their proposals would be shortly realised by Reagan.
Also, on 29 March the United States and Turkey signed an agreement
giving the United States continued rights to twelve installations that
had, since the 1976 US arms embargo, been available only through a
series of temporary accords. The reported quid pro quo was $450
million in economic and military aid.[43]

Together, these arrangements bore a superficial resemblance to the surrogate arrangements of the past. But there was a vital difference: when the United States backed the British and Iranian 'peace keeping' efforts in the Indian Ocean region, prime responsibility for both plans and action rested with the allies. America played a supplemental, albeit powerful and inspiring, role in sustaining the pro-Western order. Now the relationship was reversed: America would play the leading part with the others acting in support.

THE CARTERITES STALK THE ELUSIVE ENEMY

The Carter Persian Gulf buildup was marked by a staunch determination to make up for much lost ground in a short period of time. But it was a determination directed again toward elusive objects: like policy makers who had gone before, the Carter hawks still had trouble defining their enemy.

To be sure, there was no question, in the words of Harold Brown, that the 'leadership and resources of the Soviet Union' posed the greatest potential 'for disruption and destruction'[44] in the Persian Gulf as elsewhere. But the Soviet Union, as Brown recognised, 'was only part of the problem'. The Kremlin, despite the growing military power at its disposal, 'had tended thus far to exploit existing troubles rather than create new ones. . . . Longstanding differences among nations persist in South Asia, the Middle East, and Southern Europe. Political, economic and social grievances exist on a worldwide basis and provide fertile soil for sabotage, subversion, terror, and civil war.'[45]

One might ask rhetorically: given such an expansive view of threats to Western security, when might the United States *not* intervene? Clearly, direct Soviet intervention was one instance where the case for intervention would be clear. Indeed, the Carter administration strategy for employing the Rapid Deployment Force – a strategy inspired by the indefatigable Komer – was oriented squarely toward facing a Soviet thrust into Iran. In Komer's view, it would be impossible to defend Northern Iran from a Soviet assault. But a trip wire could be set up across the Zagros Mountains that the Soviets could be told not to pass. Such a trip wire could be established by a relatively small number of American troops getting there first. The Soviets would then have to decide whether they wished to engage US forces in combat – something both sides have avoided since 1919. History suggested that they would choose prudence. But even if they embarked on a path of adventurism, they would not have an easy time. There were 324 choke points where the Soviet advance could be stalled. Soviet numerical superiority would be partially offset by the narrow frontages on which Soviet divisions could operate in the mountains. Thus, although the Soviets could eventually overwhelm US forces in an all-out assault, the United States was far from impotent in the region; and by building a credible deterrent force could avoid over conflict with the USSR.[46]

The problem with the trip wire strategy was that it confronted the threat which was least likely to occur. As Komer noted, 'the most immediate threat to stability in the Indian Ocean area is not an overt Russian attack but rather internal instability, coups, subversion, and so forth.'[47] But although a direct Soviet military assault was not likely, it posed the greatest risk if it took place. Thus, it made sense to concentrate US resources on the most dangerous threat rather than dissipate them on trying to control events which, though undesirable, could be lived with so long as the Soviets did not interfere.

Yet the enemy still remained elusive for, as we have seen throughout, the Soviet interference that policy makers feared usually entailed measures short of direct military action. This type of interference, as Assistant Secretary of State for Near Eastern and South Asian Affairs Harold Saunders, observed, was 'less easy to characterize because the exact nature of Soviet involvement may not be so clear as it is in the case of overt military aggression'. The Soviets supported a number of governments and liberation organisations. While they might not fully control such governments or subversive movements, that was not the issue. Rather, the issue was 'whether the Soviets have positioned themselves to take advantage, for their own purposes, of situations in which the interests of both parties coincide. In many such circumstances the Soviet role would be apparent, but the degree of direct Soviet responsibility for their actions will be more difficult to determine'.[48] For example, an attack by South Yemen on the YAR might not in itself be cause for US military action: But South Yemen received Soviet bloc assistance. The US response would depend on the *extent* of Soviet, or Cuban, or East German complicity in the actions of the Aden regime.[49]

Yet the most difficult scenario – and the one most frequently drawn by Washington defence planners – was that of Iran. A weak central authority, such as prevailed after the Second World War, might be unable to control the fissiparous forces in the country. In a situation of national disintegration and upheaval, the pro-Soviet Tudeh party might seize, however briefly, the reins of power and invite Soviet aid. Or Azerbaijani, Kurdish or Baluchi separatists could set up independent republics and ask for Russian help.[50] In none of these cases would the US be obliged to confront the Soviets at the point of incursion. But Washington might well be obliged to set up the trip wire to stop any moves closer to the oil fields. If so, when would the trip wire be established? At the onset of Iran's political disintegration? Or only after Soviet forces had come in? Moreover, the environment would be one of extreme disorder. Even if US forces were in Iran only to counter Soviet hegemonism, they might provoke fierce resistance from the Iranians themselves. And there would be little Washington could do militarily to master the internal forces that would hold ultimate sway over the course of events.

And so, the administration accomplished much but also left many questions unanswered. It left them unanswered not because policy makers did not think of them, but because the situation was fluid and complex – a point summed up by the comment in the Wolfowitz Report that 'we cannot even project who will be the enemy of whom five years hence in the Middle East'.[51]

6 Reagan Takes Charge

Where Carter policy makers had trouble answering unanswerable questions, officials in the new Reagan administration did not view the answers as having much significance. Rather than worrying over objective conditions – and the constraints they imposed – Reagan officials sought to bend those conditions to American will. This brought both a heightened aggressiveness in US policy and blatant disregard for local realities. For the prime task was not to deal with those realities but to recapture respect for American power. In the words of Defense Secretary Caspar Weinberger, Washington would convey 'to the world and particularly to the Soviets, that there is indeed a new resolve in America, that President Reagan's election and his action constitute a really watershed change in American policy, and that it's no longer safe for the Soviets or anyone to regard America as weak, irresolute or divided'.[1] Once this image was conveyed, such a statement assumed, intractable problems would disappear.

The administration's resolve in the Middle East was not the product of a coherent view of the threat to US interests. Reagan himself was given to an unalloyed anti-Sovietism. 'Let's not delude ourselves,' he stated in a *Wall Street Journal* interview on 3 June 1980. 'The Soviet Union underlies all of the unrest going on. If they weren't engaged in this game of dominoes, there wouldn't be any hotspots in the world.' Others in the administration, however, articulated more conventional formulations: the Soviet Union did not necessarily underlie all the trouble in the world, but could take advantage of it nevertheless. As Weinberger explained: 'even the threats that may arise independently for various reasons are affected by Soviet power. Moreover, the Soviets sometimes choose to stimulate local instabilities, and even where they do not, they benefit from the opportunities that these instabilities offer.'[2] Furthermore, Reagan officials agreed with their predecessors' view that a direct Soviet invasion of Iran was the least likely threat to Persian Gulf stability. More likely, in the order of probability, were: internal instability; intraregional conflict; and Soviet-backed subversion or invasion by 'surrogates'.[3]

But these were not distinctions the Reaganites were really worried about. As one official said, 'the most likely threat is the pattern we are seeing today, both internal and external threats all mixed together'.[4] Distinctions, therefore, did not count. In Weinberger's view, the

95

United States would have to respond to 'threats across the entire spectrum of conflict'.[5] In the 1984–8 'Defense Guidance' paper, Pentagon planners were instructed to prepare for a direct US intervention in the Persian Gulf area 'whatever the circumstances'.[6] Indeed, in a much noted press conference statement on 1 October 1981, Reagan seemed at last to commit the United States to preserving social structures threatened by internal change: 'and Iran – I would have to say that Saudi Arabia, we will not permit to be another Iran'.[7] Lest the president's remark be viewed as completely impromptu, he elaborated on it two weeks later:

> What I had in mind was that I don't believe the Shah's government would have fallen if the United States had made it plain that we would stand by that government and support them in whatever had to be done to curb the revolution and let it be seen that we still felt that we were allied with them.[8]

Thus, Reagan policy makers eliminated the old problem of the elusive enemy. The Soviet Union, Soviet proxies, independent actors whose aims happened to coincide with Soviet aims, revolutionary elements opposed to conservative friends of the US – each was a threat to the United States. The enemy was no longer elusive because the image of it had expanded so as to be almost all-encompassing.

MILITARY ASCENDANCY

Along with a broadened concept of the enemy came a vast expansion of US military power. Referring to the defence budget as a whole, Secretary Weinberger grudgingly admitted that the Carter administration had increased real defence spending. But to Weinberger's thinking, this increase was only 'modest'. It is important to understand, he asserted on 18 March 1981, 'that the principal shortcoming of the defense budget we inherited is not so much that it omitted critical programs entirely in order to fund others, but rather that it failed to provide full funding of many programs it conceded were necessary but felt unable to afford.'

This was particularly true in respect to the Persian Gulf. Reagan defence planners immediately amended the Carter Fiscal Year 1982 request for the Rapid Deployment Force with a \$2 billion addition – representing an 85 per cent increase over the Carter 'baseline' request.[9]

This would constitute the first instalment in a substantial upgrading of the RDF. On 24 April Weinberger announced that the RDF would be transformed from a joint task force into a unified command with responsibility for the Persian Gulf. Rather than drawing from a pool of units under other operational commands, the RDF would be assigned units of its own, which would be supplemented with other forces should the need arise. Weinberger directed that this new command be set up within three to five months; the new organisation was formally constituted on 1 January 1983 under the name of Central Command.[10]

In addition to achieving higher status in the defence hierarchy, the RDF was also greatly enlarged. By the end of 1982, Reagan planners had decided to double the original Carter 'tripwire' force. They envisioned a 440 000-man RDF consisting of five army combat divisions (two-and-two-thirds more than planned under Carter), three aircraft carrier battle groups, one amphibious ready group, ten Air Force tactical fighter wings (three more than provided by the Carter programme), and two Marine Corps marine amphibious forces. Some of these forces would be 'dual-hatted with NATO' – that is, earmarked for NATO use as well as for action with the RDF. Others might be drawn from the Pacific area. If these 'dual-hatted' forces were assigned to the Central Command, US allies would have to take up the slack.[11] For in the administration's view, the threat in 'Southwest Asia' – the region of the Central Command – was of greater urgency than threats to Europe and in the Pacific. The Persian Gulf, said Weinberger, would 'be the fulcrum of conflict for the foreseeable future'.[12]

Another measure of the administration's priorities was its application of the idea of horizontal escalation to a Persian Gulf intervention. In the words of Assistant Secretary of Defense for International Security Affairs Francis J. West, the United States had to be ready to interdict a Soviet invasion, but 'would not be compelled to respond only at the Soviet point of attack'.[13] The United States, as Weinberger put it, 'must not pursue a defense strategy that anticipates a point-to-point response to these actions, but rather one which permits us to take full advantage of Soviet vulnerabilities'.[14] A wartime strategy that confronted the Soviets with the risk of an American counteroffensive against its vulnerable points would enhance deterrence and serve 'the defensive peacetime strategy'.[15]

THE STRATEGIC CONSENSUS

Reagan defence planning for the Persian Gulf had the diplomatic corollary of the 'strategic consensus' – a military grouping of America's 'friends' in the region – Pakistan, Turkey, Egypt, Israel, Jordan, Saudi Arabia and the Gulf emirates. In early 1981, Secretary of State Alexander Haig set about in search of this consensus, which he defined not as a structured alliance, but as an 'unofficial and nonspecific arrangement to counter Soviet influence in the region'.[16] His goal, he noted, would be to strengthen political and military ties with pro-Western states so as to solidify an anti-Soviet front. He would not press for a resumption of the stalled Egyptian–Israeli West Bank autonomy talks, nor a halt to further Jewish settlements that were making the negotiations irrelevant in any event. 'Strategic reality', in his view, would render such mere local issues to secondary importance.[17]

Here, he mirrored Reagan's own belief, stated during the election campaign, that the United States should not pressure Israel on the Palestinian question. And despite what the Saudis said about the need for a Palestinian settlement, Reagan asserted, their rhetoric was not to be taken seriously: they were really much more concerned about blocking Soviet expansion in the Persian Gulf. To this end, they would be natural participants, along with Egypt, Israel and the United States, in a de facto regional alliance.[18]

REGIONAL BASES

The notion that Washington could forge a strategic consensus went hand-in-glove with the idea that it would be possible to gain acquiescence in a direct US ground presence in the area. Diego Garcia was, as we have seen, the hub of the US logistics network in the Indian Ocean basin. The Carter administration enhanced the network by gaining access to facilities in Kenya, Somalia and Oman. Beyond this, Carter planners counted on being able to use Saudi bases once emergencies arose. The Saudis, after all, had 'overbuilt' their military infrastructure, and could accomodate a US intervention force. But Carter administration policy makers knew that any formal arrangments would arouse political opposition in the kingdom, and that the United States should simply assume that the facilities would be available without speaking words to that effect.

The Reaganites, however, believed that 'strategic reality' would override the 'mere' local politics. From the very early days of the administration, spokesmen made clear the desire for a ground-based US presence. Diego Garcia, once seen as a means of avoiding tenuous reliance on continental bases, would become one element of a strategy that combined navalism with oldstyle garrison deployment. 'The fact is,' asserted Deputy Secretary of Defense Frank Carlucci, 'that for the most effective deterrent we need both sea-based and land-based forces'.[19] The reluctance of local regimes to provide domicile for such forces did not daunt him. While the United States did not currently have access, this 'does not mean that we won't always have that kind of access'. For 'once our determination becomes clear to our friends and allies in the Middle East, they will become more forthcoming on the kinds of access that we need'.[20]

THE SHORTCOMINGS OF WILL

The administration would have no luck in obtaining either the strategic consensus or the forward land bases in the Persian Gulf. For contrary to the Reaganite metaphysic of 'will', 'mere' local realities were not readily swept away simply because the US wanted them to be.

The fact that Israel and conservative Arab states had the same patron did not provide enough common ground for making friends of inveterate enemies. The Saudis remained unconvinced, despite much US exhortation, that the Soviet Union was a greater threat to them than Israel. (Nor did they obligingly play down the Palestinian issue.)[21] US efforts to reinforce military ties with all its assorted 'friends' divided these friends rather than uniting them. In particular, Washington's announcement on 6 March 1981 that it would sell 'enhancement' gear – auxiliary fuel tanks, bomb racks and advanced Sidewinder air-to-air missiles – for sixty-two Saudi F-15 aircraft roused strong objections by Israel, despite the concurrent offer to the Israelis of $600 million in additional credits over the next two years; Israeli objections then became furious when the administration followed that by deciding in April to sell AWACS reconnaissance planes to the Saudis. The Israelis did nothing to further the goal of pro-Western unity with their 7 June 1981 attack of the Iraqi nuclear facility in Baghdad – an act that spread fear throughout the Arab Middle East; a month later they commenced a bombing campaign into Lebanon. The United States seemed to acquiesce in both actions, responding with a temporary suspension of warplane deliveries to Israel – a mere slap on the wrist because the sanctions were lifted on 17 August.

Indeed, the only tangible result of Washington's search for a strategic consensus was a bilateral US–Israeli agreement, signed on 30 November. This accord – the so-called 'memorandum of understanding' – provided for creation of working groups to discuss: 1) joint Israeli–US exercises in the Eastern Mediterranean; 2) establishment of joint maintenance facilities and infrastructure; 3) co-operation in research and development and in defence training.[22] Coming so soon on the heels of the Israeli attack in Iraq and Lebanon, such an arrangement looked more like the framework for a US–Israeli alliance than a strategic understanding among pro-Western states in the region. In any event, it did not last. On 14 December the Israeli Knesset voted to annex the Golan Heights. Washington responded on 19 December by suspending the memorandum of understanding.[23]

And just as simple US 'determination' did not suffice to create a strategic consensus that did not exist, neither did such determination make conservative Arab states more willing to admit dependence on the United States or to accept a US presence on their soil. Indeed, in what the administration should have considered a rebuke of its insistences on forward bases, the Gulf Co-operation Council, formally constituted on 25 May 1981 to promote economic, social and security co-operation among the Arab Gulf states (Saudi Arabia, Kuwait, Bahrain, Qatar, United Arab Emirates and Oman), called for common defence efforts based on nonalignment. In November, Oman, to avoid criticism from other member states, was forced to ask the United States to scale down a scheduled Marine landing exercise on Omani shores.[24]

Even Anwar Sadat, America's closest Arab friend, quarrelled with Washington over the terms of collaboration. While continuing its offer to give US forces access to Ras Banas, he balked at signing a formal written agreement to that effect, thus delaying congressional appropriation of the $400 million the Defense Department wanted for upgrading the base.[25]

Sadat's assassination by Islamic fundamentalists on 6 October 1981 might have served as an object lesson of the perils of getting too close – at least too obviously close – to the United States. It might also have dealt a blow to Washington's strategic plans. As it was, US luck held: the successor regime of Hosni Mubarak did not break from the pro-American orbit. But the dispute over Ras Banas continued. By the spring of 1983 talks had reached impasse over Cairo's demand that Egypt control base construction rather than turning the work over to the US Army Corps of Engineers.[26]

THE LEBANON MORASS

In an address delivered on 26 May 1982 to the Chicago Council on Foreign Relations, Secretary of State Alexander Haig seemed to retreat from the military metaphysic that had dominated US policy to date. He departed from the administration's relative disregard for the Arab–Israeli conflict and regional issues. He appeared, moreover, to tone down the single-minded anti-Sovietism that had characterised the earlier pronouncements. There were, he said, three main issues to be addressed by US diplomacy: the Iran–Iraq War (then in its twentieth month); the Palestinian autonomy negotiations; and the Lebanon crisis. Of the Iran–Iraq War he said, 'there is great risk that the conflict may spill over into neighboring states. It may lead to unforeseen and far-reaching changes in the regional balance of power.' Turning to the autonomy talks, he affirmed the necessity to go beyond a bilateral Egyptian–Israeli peace and to resolve 'the Palestinian problem in all its aspects'. In a thinly veiled attack at Israeli settlements policy on the West Bank he declared: 'Unilateral actions by any party that attempt to prejudge or bias the final outcome of the process serve only to raise suspicions and aggravate relationships.' Finally, he singled out the Lebanon crisis as a 'focal point of danger'. He followed this with an assertion which proved more true than he probably realised at the time: 'All of those conditions are present in abundance that might be ignited into a war with far-reaching consequences.'[27]

Yet, at the same time as Haig adopted what one observer hailed as a 'shifting, more realistic perception',[28] he was being informed by Israeli officials of plans to invade Lebanon. Haig's tacit acceptance of these plans nullified his talk of pursuing a more ambitious diplomacy. The war itself revealed the inadequacies of a strategy that focused on Persian Gulf defence and gave short shrift to the Arab–Irsraeli dispute.

In late July 1981, the Israelis and PLO agreed to a Southern Lebanon ceasefire, negotiated through US and Saudi intermediaries. Israeli Defence Minister Ariel Sharon, however, had no intention of observing an indefinite ceasefire: he planned to mount a massive invasion of Lebanon to finish off the PLO. The United States knew of his designs – and knew, moreover, that they went beyond Southern Lebanon. Before launching the invasion, Sharon met with Haig in May 1982. Rather than remonstrating with the Israeli Defence Minister, Haig indicated that the United States would not really mind a limited strike against the PLO provided the Israelis awaited an appropriate provocation to break the ceasefire. Such an attitude was not out of form: Reagan policy makers considered the PLO an ally of the Soviets and wished to reduce, if not eliminate, PLO and Syrian influence in Lebanon.[29]

The pretext was provided on 3 June, when a Palestinian splinter group attempted, unsuccessfully, to assassinate the Israeli ambassador in London. The PLO had ejected this group for extremism, and PLO leaders were among its targets. But Israel was not interested in such subtleties.

The Israelis struck on 6 June. Within four days, they had driven to the outskirts of Beirut. Washington's reaction was less than assertive. In one breath, US officials demanded a ceasefire accompanied by immediate Israeli withdrawal; Special Envoy Philip Habib, who had helped negotiate the July 1981 truce, was sent into the area to work out a new cessation of hostilities. But in the next breath, they justified the Israeli move by accusing the Palestinians of using Southern Lebanon as a launching pad for attacks on Israel – even though the PLO had observed the ceasefire there for over ten months. Then, with Israeli troops outside Beirut, Haig and his associates trumpeted their belief that US interests were well served by the Israeli cleanout of the PLO. The Israeli government, they implied, might have actually done the US a favour by ignoring American demands for a military pullback: for the drive on Beirut had created new conditions in which long-held US objectives – the establishment of a strong Lebanese central government and concomitant reduction of Syrian and PLO strength – could finally be realised. In a talk with reporters on 7 June, Haig had foreshadowed this reasoning. Referring to *Israeli* losses, he stated that 'we [had] lost an aircraft and helicopter yesterday'.[30]

Reagan himself did not assert his will until his reputedly outraged 12 August phone call to Israeli Prime Minister Menachem Begin, which brought an end to Israel's devastating bombing raids on West Beirut. In the meanwhile, Haig had resigned on 25 June because of both personality and policy differences with other figures in the Reagan entourage. Weinberger and National Security Advisor William Clark favoured rebuking Israel for the invasion, whereas Haig had come to a practically open alignment with Israeli aims. Moreover, Haig wanted to use pressure of a possible Israeli attack on West Beirut to push the PLO out of the city. At the same time, Clark was assuring the Saudis that Israeli forces would not advance against the PLO-occupied part of Beirut.[31] Amidst these difficulties Reagan announced the appointment of George Shultz as Haig's successor.

At the outset, Shultz seemed to abandon the military focus of administration policy, by which Western oil security was a function of US power in the Indian Ocean and Persian Gulf. Rather, in an outlook reminiscent of the early Eisenhower years, Shultz emphasised the need to resolve the Arab–Israeli conflict. This meant dealing squarely with the Palestinian issue as a priority of US diplomacy. As he stated in his confirmation hearings, held on 13 and 14 July, 'the crisis in Lebanon makes painful and totally clear a central reality of the Middle East: the legitimate needs and problems of the Palestinian people must be addressed and resolved, urgently in all their dimensions'.[32]

Shultz's views strongly influenced the president's 1 September speech on the Middle East. In this speech Reagan called for a 'fresh start' that recognised the realities of the situation. He proposed a peace programme that for the first time placed the issue of Palestinian rights at the very centre of US diplomacy.

Reagan began the speech with a sense of exaltation over recent self-proclaimed accomplishments in the Middle East. On the day of the speech, PLO fighters had completed their evacuation of Beirut under supervision of a multinational force that included a US Marine contingent. The evacuation accord had been negotiated through Special Envoy Habib, whom Reagan praised for 'heroic' work.

But in the president's view, efforts toward peace could not end with Lebanon. Tragic as it was, the Lebanon war had 'left us with a new opportunity for Middle East peace'. Reagan sought to exploit this opportunity by offering a plan proposing Palestinian autonomy on the West Bank of the Gaza Strip in an entity linked to Jordan. He called for Israel to cease settlement activity; and declared that the United States would accept no solution involving Israeli annexation or permanent control. He larded the address with compassion for the Palestinian plight. The Beirut exodus, he said, 'dramatizes more than ever the homelessness of the Palestinian people.'[33]

The 'Jordan option' supported by Reagan did not recognise the key Palestinian demand, affirmed by the Arab League at Fez on 9 September, for an independent state under PLO leadership. Furthermore, it made no provision for the now 2.5 million Palestinians of the diaspora. Nevertheless, Arab League leaders did not reject his proposal or condemn America. Instead they made a positive counter-proposal that offered explicit recognition of Israel in return for a Palestinian state on West Bank and Gaza Strip. For it was now apparent that the only way to achieve even the minimal goal of saving the West Bank from Israeli annexation was to play along with the United States.

Israel, however, flatly rejected the Reagan initiative. This left Washington facing the dilemma of how hard to press Israel to negotiate a Palestinian settlement, and how to stop the Israelis from achieving a fait accompli with accelerated West Bank settlement.

The administration faced the dilemma by turning away from it. Shultz quickly announced that the administration had no intention of withholding economic or military assistance to force Israeli compromise. As he stated on 5 September: 'We don't have any plans to try to maneuver people into a peace negotiation by talking about withholding aid or anything like that.' Insofar as pressure would figure in US diplomacy, it would be the passive pressure arising 'from the possibility of peace'.[34]

With such feeble impetus behind it, the initiative was stymied.

In mid-September, Christian militia units slaughtered Palestinian civilians in a bloody 36-hour rampage through the Sabra and Shatila refugee camps. The action was abetted by Israeli forces encircling the camps. It was indirectly abetted by the United States, which, by withdrawing the last Marines on 10 September, violated its pledge to PLO Chairman Yasser Arafat to guarantee the safety of Palestinian civilians left behind in West Beirut.

The refugee tragedy could have served as a political godsend to Washington if it had been used to justify putting pressure on Israel to make a bargain on Palestinian rights. But it was not. Less than a week after the refugee slaughter, administration spokesmen adopted a 'quieter tone' in their statements on the Lebanon conflict – deliberately, they said, to avoid a break with Begin that would impede eventual progress toward a general peace.[35] Such a quietness of tone had been suggested already when Washington asked Israeli permission to send US Marines back to Beirut.[36] A continuing resolution by an adjournment conscious Congress kept aid for Israel flowing at previous levels; and State Department officials again denied that any cutback was contemplated. On 24 September Vice President George Bush scolded the Arab League for offering only implicit recognition of Israel: that, he said, was 'not enough'.[37]

Thus, lacking any reason for Israel to change its mind, the Reagan autonomy plan was dead from the moment the Israeli government rejected it. It retained artificial life only because the PLO and Jordan continued to discuss the terms on which King Hussein might represent the PLO if talks with Israel ever occurred. These PLO–Jordanian discussions broke down on 10 April 1983, after a provisional accord reached between Arafat and Hussein was spurned by other PLO leaders. American inability to halt Israeli settlements was an important factor in the rupture of PLO–Jordanian contact: once it became clear that participation in the Reagan scheme held no promise of ending the Israeli occupation, the PLO had no incentive for abdicating its leadership role to King Hussein.

The autonomy plan dead, Secretary Shultz rushed off to the Middle East to bury it. In early May, he prevailed on the Israeli and Lebanese governments to agree to an arrangement whereby Israeli forces would be withdrawn from Lebanon – if, that is, the Syrians (who had not been made part of the proceedings) would agree to do likewise. The accord relieved Israel of any pressure whatever to go further toward comprehensive settlement. In essence, it obliged the Lebanese army to help suppress PLO activity in Southern Lebanon. For the first two years of the pact, Israelis would participate in joint patrols with Lebanese forces. And the southernmost part of Lebanon would be patrolled by the Israeli-sponsored militia forces of Major Saed Haddad.[38]

Such an agreement could only mark the end of efforts to deal with the plight of the Palestinians. Nonetheless, on the strength of it, Shultz announced that F–16 deliveries – held up in late March to spur Israeli withdrawal from Lebanon – would be resumed. On 14 June Defense Secretary Weinberger announced United States willingness to revive the US–Israeli 'memorandum of understanding'.[39]

There was now no suggestion that Palestinian autonomy ranked high on the Reagan agenda. Shultz had gone the way of his predecessors – recognising, even the most hawkish of administrations, the necessity of an overall peace, but unable, once again, to transform recognition into reality.

CONCLUSION

As a result, the administration was left without any comprehensive strategy for the Middle East. It was left, rather, with an expanded version of the Indian Ocean military strategy devised years before.

Already, in the 1960s, that strategy was inappropriate to the circumstances. Then as now, the complex problems of the area defied military solutions. By the 1980s, however, events have made it not only inappropriate but increasingly dangerous. For while US administrations have a long history of pursuing policies that are inappropriate to the circumstances, they have been able to do so because of a favourable combination of power and luck. That combination might not last. As power becomes irrelevant, there is the high risk that luck will fail.

List of Abbreviations

DDRS   Declassified Documents Reference System, microfilm collection

DEF   Department of State, Bureau of Politico-Military Affairs records, Washington, DC

FRUS   *Foreign Relations of the United States* (Washington, DC: USGPO)

NSC   National Security Council records, microfilm collection

PM   Department of the Navy, Political-Military Policy Branch records, Naval Archives, Washington, DC

SPD   Department of the Navy, Strategic Plans Division records, Naval Archives, Washington, DC

Notes and References

Introduction

1. *Public Papers of the Presidents of the United States: Jimmy Carter, 1980– 81* (Washington, DC: USGPO, 1981) p. 195.
2. Ibid., p. 197.
3. *Foreign Relations of the United States (FRUS), 1948* (Washington, DC: USGPO, 1974) 5: 47.
4. Memorandum by the Secretary of the Interior and Petroleum Administrator for Defense, 'National Security Problems Concerning Free World Petroleum Demand and Potential Supplies', 8 December 1952, NSC 138.
5. Robert H. Ferrell (ed.), *The Eisenhower Diaries* (New York: W. W. Norton, 1981) p. 319.
6. Eisenhower to Winston Churchill, 29 March 1956, quoted in Donald Neff, *Warriors at Suez: Eisenhower Takes America into the Middle East* (New York: Simon & Schuster, 1981) p. 282.
7. See note 4 above (quotes); see also *FRUS*, 1950, 5: 240–1.
8. *FRUS*, 1949, 6: 39.
9. *FRUS*, 1950, 5: 218, 231 (quote).
10. Steering group on preparations for talks between the president and Winston Churchill, 'Middle East Negotiation Paper', 31 December 1951, DDRS (78) 282C.
11. Report by the Secretaries of State and Defense and the Director for Mutual Security, 'Reexamination of United States Programs for National Security', Part Four, 19 January 1953, NSC 141.
12. The words were those of Robert Pranger, Deputy Assistant Secretary of Defense (International Security Affairs), US, Congress, House Subcommittee on National Security Policy and Scientific Developments, Committee on Foreign Affairs, *The Indian Ocean: Political and Strategic Future*, 92nd Congress, 1st session, 1971, p. 170.
13. Memorandum prepared in the office of the Assistant Secretary of Defense (Program Analysis and Evaluation), 'Capabilities for Limited Contingencies in the Persian Gulf', 15 June 1979, pp. I–20. This report was popularly known as the 'Wolfowitz Report'.

1 America Moves into the Middle East

1. Report prepared by State Department Office of Intelligence Research, 'The British Position in the Middle East', 2 October 1952, DDRS, (78) 415A.
2. Ibid.
3. State Department briefing for the president, 'Bermuda Meeting – December 4–6, 1953: Memorandum on Relative U.S.–U.K. Roles in the Middle East', 27 November 1953, DDRS, (77) 237E.

4. Memorandum of conversation with the president, 21 November 1956, DDRS, (78) 451A.

5. For a description of the proposed functioning of the Middle East Command, see negotiating paper by steering group on preparations for talks between the President and Prime Minister Churchill, 'Middle East Command', 4 January 1952, DDRS, (77) 67E.

6. [State Department?] memorandum to Eisenhower, 'Defense of the Middle East', [July?] 1955, DDRS, (78) 283A; Report by the Joint Strategic Plans Committee to the Joint Chiefs of Staff, 'U.K. Views Regarding the Middle East', JSPC 883/78, 11 August 1955, DDRS, (78) 366A; memorandum by Office of Foreign Military Affairs (Department of Defense) to Eisenhower, 'Middle East Areas', 5 May 1955, DDRS, (81) 37A (quote); Note by JCS Secretariat to holders of JCS 1887/117, 7 December 1955, DDRS, (78) 367A; Report by the Joint Middle East Planning Committee to the Joint Chiefs of Staff', Baghdad Pact Planning Staff Study . . .' JCS 1887/302, DDRS, (78) 367A.

7. JSPC 883/78, see note 6 above; Joint Chiefs of Staff memorandum, 'Logistic Support of Our Strategy in the Middle East', 12 August 1955, DDRS, (78) 367B.

8. [State Department?] memorandum to Eisenhower, DDRS, (78) 283A, note 6 above; Eden talks, Washington, 30 January–1 February 1956, memorandum of conversation, 30 January 1956, DDRS, (78) 283B; memorandum of conversation with the president, 20 December 1956, DDRS, (81) 391B.

9. See JCS comments on Iraq in memorandum, 'Logistic Support of our Strategy in the Middle East', note 7 above; see also Dulles's remarks on the 'unstable and weak situation in Iraq' in State Department memorandum of conversation with the president, 15 June 1958, DDRS, (81) 371B. The State Department intelligence report, note 1 above, adverted to a shift of power from the 'feudal oligarchy' to an 'emerging middle sector' of Iraqi society, which had grown with the spread of secular education and urbanisation. This shift, the report asserted, was 'part of a broad historical process, encouraged by factors which are integral to social and economic development'.

10. Eden talks, memorandum of conversation, 30 January 1956, note 8 above.

11. Ibid.; Eisenhower staff notes no. 62, 9 January 1957, DDRS, (79) 219C; Department of State memorandum of conversation with King Hussein, 25 March 1959, DDRS, (79) 196A; National Security Council Memorandum, 'U.S. Policy Toward the Near East', 17 June 1960, NSC 6011.

12. Memorandum of conference with the president, 24 July 1958, DDRS, (77) 355A.

13. John Foster Dulles, memorandum of conversation, 21 October 1955, DDRS (81) 217D.

14. See note 3 above.

15. Robert H. Ferrell (ed.) *The Eisenhower Diaries* (New York: W. W. Norton, 1981) p. 318.

16. US Department of State, *American Foreign Policy, 1950–1955: Basic Documents* (Washington, DC:USGPO, 1957): 2176–80.

17. For a treatment of the Anderson Mission, see Donald Neff, *Warriors at Suez: Eisenhower Takes America into the Middle East* (New York: Simon & Schuster, 1981), pp. 130–6, 168–9; see also Eisenhower diary entries for 11 January and 13 March 1956, in Ferrell, *The Eisenhower Diaries*, pp. 307–8, 318–19.

18. NSC 6011, see note 11 above.

19. *Public Papers of the Presidents of the United States: D. Eisenhower, 1957* (Washington: USGPO, 1958): 13–14.

20. 'The Middle East Resolution, approved March 9, 1957', in US, Congress, Senate Committee on Foreign Relations, *A Select Chronology and Background Documents Relating to the Middle East*, 94th Congress, 1st session, 1975, pp. 216–18.

21. *American Foreign Policy: Current Documents, 1957*: 1023–8.

22. Briefing sheet prepared by the Joint Middle East Planning Committee for the Joint Chiefs of Staff special meeting, 18 February 1957, DDRS, (79) 375A (quote); report by the Joint Middle East Planning Committee to the Joint Chiefs of Staff, 'Military Action in Relation to the Jordanian Situation', 19 February 1957, DDRS, (79) 375A; memorandum prepared in Office of Chief Naval Operations for the Secretary of the Navy, 'Financial Crisis in Jordan', 20 June 1957, DDRS, (70) 376A.

23. National Security Council Memorandum, 'U.S. Policy Toward the Near East', 4 November 1958, NSC 5820/1. Military action to protect European oil supplies was suggested only as a last resort and with the recognition that 'this course . . . could not be indefinitely pursued'.

24. The correspondence is printed in *Department of State Bulletin*, 29 (20 July 1953): 74–7.

25. The exchange was officially released, along with the January messages, on 9 July, in both Tehran and Washington.

26. Barry Rubin, *Paved with Good Intentions: The American Experience and Iran* (New York: Oxford University Press, 1980) pp. 54–90, 94–6; *Public Papers of the Presidents: Eisenhower, 1953*, 579–81.

27. Dwight D. Eisenhower, *The White House Years: Mandate for Change, 1953–1956* (Garden City, NY: Doubleday, 1963) p. 163.

28. US, Congress, *Senate Committee on Foreign Relations, Executive Sessions of the Senate Foreign Relations Committee*, 83rd Congress, 1st session, 1953 (Washington DC: USGPO, 1977) 5: 384–7.

29. Eisenhower, *The White Years: Waging Peace, 1956–1961* (Garden City, NY: Doubleday, 1965) p. 266.

30. Robert Murphy, *Diplomat Among Warriors* (Garden City, NY: Doubleday, 1964) p. 404.

31. Department of State memorandum of conversation with the President, 15 June 1958, DDRS, (81) 371B.

32. Ibid. (quotes); Eisenhower, *Waging Peace*, p. 265.

33. Eisenhower, *Waging Peace*, p. 276; Department of State to US Embassy, Beirut, 19 June 1958, DDRS, (77) 134C; Department of State memorandum of conversation between the Secretary of State and the Ambassador of Italy, 25 June 1958, DDRS, (76) 101A; see also note 31 above.

34. Briefing Notes by Allen Dulles, Meeting at the White House with

Congressional Leaders, 14 July 1958, DDRS, (79) 12D (quote); Department of State to all US Diplomatic Posts, 14 July 1958, DDRS, (77) 134G; Department of State to US Embassy, Paris, 14 July 1958, DDRS, (76) 101H.

35. Eisenhower, *Waging Peace*, p. 270.
36. *Public Papers of the Presidents: Eisenhower, 1958*: 555.
37. Memorandum of conference with the president, 24 July 1958, DDRS, (77) 355A. The Lebanon affair ended on a note of irony. In early June, President Nasser had contacted the United States with a three part formula for pacifying Lebanon: a) Chamoun would serve out his term (which expired on 28 September); b) Lebanese army commander General Fuad Chehab would become president; c) the opposition would be granted amnesty. Washington forwarded the proposal to Chamoun without endorsement, for as Dulles explained in a cable to Beirut, the United States would not 'become accomplice with Nasser' in anything the Lebanese government did not want. Chamoun obliged by ignoring Nasser's initiative. Now, after the intervention in July, US envoy Robert Murphy brokered a settlement remarkably similar to the Nasser plan; a) Chamoun would finish out his term; b) the Chamber of Deputies would elect General Chehab to succeed him; and c) the new regime would pursue a policy of conciliation. So with respect to Lebanese internal politics, the outcome of the intervention was a solution that might have been achieved five or six weeks earlier with the co-operation of arch-enemy, Nasser. Moreover, Eisenhower had never fully appreciated the moderating role played by General Chehab. A Christian like Chamoun, Chehab had refused to order the army into offensive action against the Moslem rebels for fear of splitting his troops on religious lines and igniting full-scale confessional war. For Eisenhower, however, Chehab was derelict in his duty and should have been fired. Had the firing occurred, and a more aggressive commander put in Chehab's place, Murphy might not have achieved such success in sponsoring the political settlement that Nasser had largely devised; Department of State to US Embassy, Beirut, 11 June 1958, DDRS, (81) 371A; State Department report of the history of the Lebanon crisis prior to 25 June 1958, DDRS, (76) 100J; Meeting at the White House with Congressional Leaders, 14 July 1958, note 34 above.
38. Minutes, bipartisan leadership meeting, 12 August 1956, DDRS, (76) 217B.
39. Eisenhower, *Waging Peace*, p. 50.
40. Memorandum of conference with the president, 29 October 1956, 7.15pm, DDRS, (78) 449D (quote); Memorandum of conference with the president, 29 October 1956, 8.15pm, DDRS, (78) 450A.
41. Eisenhower to Dulles (in Paris), 12 December 1956, DDRS, (76) 217D.
42. Eisenhower diary entries for 11 January and 8 March 1956, in Ferrell, *The Eisenhower Diaries*, pp. 307–8, 318–9 (quote).
43. Eisenhower diary entry for 28 March 1956, Ferrell, *The Eisenhower Diaries*, pp. 323–4; memorandum by Dulles to the president, 'Near Eastern Policies', 28 March 1956, DDRS, (80) 302B (quote).

2 The Strategic Formulation

1. Memorandum by Admiral Roy L. Johnson, 'Long Range Objectives 1968–73', Command File, Post 1 Jan 46, Serial 0055P93, 5 September 1958.

2. Memorandum prepared by Long Range Objectives Group, 'Factors Affecting Changes in the Power Position in Areas Bordering the Southern Oceans (Indian Ocean, South Atlantic)', PM 5710, Serial 0079P93, 31 May 1960.

3. Memorandum prepared by Long Range Objectives Group to CNO (Admiral Arleigh Burke), 'Assuring a Future Base Structure in the African Indian Ocean Area', PM 5710, Serial 0092P93, 27 June 1960 (quote); memorandum prepared by Long Range Objectives Group, 'Study of the Feasibility and Cost of Maintaining Continuous Balanced Deployments in the Indian Ocean 1961–1965', PM 5710 Serial 00125P93, 25 August 1960; see also note 2 above.

4. 'Factors Affecting Changes in Power Position. . .' Serial 0079P93, note 2 above (quote); 'Assuring a Future Base Structure. . .', Serial 0092P93, note 3 above.

5. 'Assuring a Future Base Structure. . .', Serial 0092P93, note 3 above.

6. See note 2 above.

7. 'Study of the Feasibility. . .', Serial 00125P93, note 3 above.

8. See note 1 above (quote); see also note 2.

9. This was the view of Stuart Barber, the top civilian in the Long Range Objectives Group; see also Admiral Miles H. Hubbard to CNO, SPD 1961/5010, Serial 0015P04B, 15 August 1961.

10. Memorandum by Burke to Op–06 (Deputy CNO, Plans, Policy and Operations), 'Indian Ocean Fleet', SPD 1961 Serials, Op–00 Memo 00152–61, 6 March 1961.

11. Memorandum prepared by Strategic Plans Division analysing JCS document 'Estimate of the Military Posture Throughout the Free World, FY 1956 Through FY 1959', SPD, 1954, file A16–12, Serial 00431P30, 17 May 1954; memorandum prepared by Strategic Plans Division, Navy submission for Periodic Report to Secretary of Defense, 'The Status of U.S. Programs for National Security (as of 30 June 1954)', SPD, 1954, file A 16–1.

12. See note 1 above.

13. Memorandum prepared by Long Range Objectives Group, 'Long Range Objectives Through 1973', Command File Post 1 Jan 46, Serial 0060P93, 9 May 1962.

14. 'Assuring a Future Base Structure. . .', Serial 0092P93, note 3 above.

15. 'Study of the Feasibility. . .', Serial 00125P93, note 3 above.

16. 'Assuring a Future Base Structure. . .', Serial 0092P93.

17. CINCUSNAVEUR to Department of the Navy, PM/Indian Ocean 25 February 64 to 30 September 65, Naval Message R 0714462, September 1965.

18. These incidents are described in 'Western Pacific and Indian Ocean Base Study', Final Report, June 1968, SPD/Series XVII/Miscellaneous Plans and Studies, v. 2, ch. 2. This report was part of a 'World Wide Base

Study' Robert S. McNamara requested in order to force the services to justify both the existing US base structure and the plans they had for future bases.

19. Memorandum prepared by Op–611 (Africa, Middle East, and South Asia Policy Branch), 'Comments on Political Annex, Westpac Base Study', PM/Indian Ocean 1 October 65 to —, Op–611/isb, 2 January 1968.

20. Memorandum prepared by Op–61 (Politico-Military Policy Branch), 'Establishment of a Minimum Fleet Support Facility on Diego Garcia', PM/Indian Ocean 1 October 65 to —, Op–61F8/gsh, February 1966.

21. See note 18 above.

22. See note 19 above.

23. 'Western Pacific and Indian Ocean Base Study', v. 2, app. B and v. 3, ch. 1 (quote). See note 18 above.

24. Ibid.

3 Kennedy, the Arabs and the Navy's New Frontier

1. John F. Kennedy, *The Strategy of Peace*, Allan Nevins (ed.) (New York: Harper, 1960) p. 65.

2. Ibid., p. 183.

3. Ibid., p. 71.

4. Address delivered to 50th Anniversary Dinner of B'nai Zion, New York City, 9 February 1958, quoted in Zionist Organization of America (ed.), *John F. Kennedy on Israel, Zionism and Jewish Issues* (New York: Herzl Press, 1965) p. 45.

5. Kennedy, *Strategy of Peace*, p. 111.

6. Ibid., pp. 107, 114 (quote).

7. Ibid., p. 105.

8. Ibid., p. 186.

9. Ibid., preface.

10. Letter printed in *New York Times*, 26 June 1961, p. 2.

11. Kennedy made his remarks in an interview granted during the 1960 presidential campaign, with Dr Jacob Rubin of the Israeli newspaper *HaBoker*. See *John F. Kennedy, Zionism and Jewish Issues*, p. 57. See also, *Strategy of Peace*, p. 117.

12. On 1 June 1961, Israeli Prime Minister David Ben Gurion reported that he had found 'a large measure of agreement' in talks with President Kennedy on the refugee issue. He added that 'in no way was I disappointed'. *New York Times*, 2 June 1961, pp. 1, 3.

13. See *New York Times*, 26 November 1961, pp. 1, 21; *New York Times*, 6 December 1961, p. 8; *New York Times*, 20 December 1961, p. 10; *New York Times*, 9 June 1962, p. 6; *New York Times*, 19 December 1962, p. 3; *New York Times*, 3 October 1962, p. 5. Dr Johnson proposed a settlement that emphasised resettlement and economic development as opposed to repatriation of the Palestinians. The only proposal that departed from Kennedy's was his idea of polling the Palestinians to determine their preference regarding resettlement or repatriation. This had no appeal as a compromise, because the refugees would not be

guaranteed their first choice, and in any case a low ceiling would have been set on the number the Israelis would let in. Johnson's scheme, then, was no real departure from the Kennedy–Ben Gurion position.

14.   Bowles (Adis Ababa) to Department of State, 21 February 1962, printed in Mordechai Gazit, *President Kennedy's Policy toward the Arab States and Israel* (Tel Aviv: The Shiloah Center for Middle Eastern and African Studies, 1983) pp. 74–83.

15.   Ibid., pp. 18–21.

16.   Kennedy's assurances to the Saudis were made public on 8 January 1963. See *New York Times*, 9 January 1963, p. 1.

17.   For the key passages in the letter, see Mohamed Heikal, *The Cairo Documents* (Garden City, NY: Doubleday, 1973) pp. 216–7.

18.   Ibid., pp. 222–3.

19.   Ibid., p. 222.

20.   Memorandum by McGeorge Bundy, 'Indian Ocean Naval Deployment', 19 March 1964, National Security Action Memorandum No. 289; 'Western Pacific and Indian Ocean Base Study', Final Report, June 1968, SPD/Series XVII/Miscellaneous Plans and Studies, v. 2, ch. 3; Department of State to US Embassy, London, 21 January 1964, DEF 1 IND; a summary of Indian Ocean development is found in the Navy Department memorandum, 'Indian Ocean Naval Force', PM/Indian Ocean, 1 October 65 to —, Serial 0037P61, 30 August 1967. The April–May cruise was by the *Bon Homme Richard* carrier group; the August–September exercise featured an appearance by the *Enterprise*.

21.   Memorandum by Jeffrey C. Kitchen to U. Alexis Johnson, 'Proposed Note to the British Government Concerning Possible Long-Term Development of Base Facilities in the Indian Ocean Area', 25 April 1963, DEF 15 UK–US.

22.   Ibid.

23.   Joint State–Defense memorandum, 'Defense Problems in the Indian Ocean Area', transmitted in Department of State to US Embassy, London, 21 January 1964, DEF 1 IND.

24.   'U.S. Defense Interests in the Indian Ocean. Memorandum of U.K./ U.S. London Discussions, February 1964', transmitted in Kitchen to Dean Rusk, 3 March 1964, DEF 15 IND–US.

25.   Kohler to Vance, 7 December 1966, DEF 15 IND–US.

26.   Ibid.

27.   Kitchen to Rusk, 17 August 1965, DEF 15 IND–US.

28.   See note 3 above.

29.   Quoted in Phillip Darby, *British Defence Policy East of Suez, 1946–1968* (London: Oxford University Press, 1973) pp. 284–5.

30.   See note 4 above; see also memorandum by Guy A. Lee, 'Mr. Kitchen's Meeting re Indian Ocean bases', 3 January 1964, DEF 15 IND–US.

31.   See note 5 above.

32.   See note 4 above.

33.   See note 5 above.

34.   The Diego Garcia proposal resembled two other key projects of the McNamara Pentagon – the C–5A transport aircraft and the Fast Deployment Logistics (FDL) ships. Both were designed to permit

deployments of centrally located 'mobile fire brigade' reserves to world trouble spots. The C–5A, though plagued by cost overruns and technical difficulties, is presently in service. The FDL ships would have provided floating arsenals, capable of transporting tanks, trucks, personnel carriers and artillery, as well as ammunition and rations. They would have been located in strategic waters throughout the world, to be sent to crisis spots where they would 'marry up' with troops brought in by air. The FDL was scuttled because of Congressional opposition arising from the Vietnam experience. It last appeared in Lyndon Johnson's final (Fiscal Year 1970) defence budget.

35.　Memorandum by Jeffrey C. Kitchen to Dean Rusk, 'Indian Ocean Islands: British Interest in U.S. Financial Contribution', 17 August 1965, DEF 15 IND–US.

36.　Memorandum by Jeffrey C. Kitchen to Dean Rusk, 'Discussions with the British on Indian Ocean Islands and Related Topics', 11 February 1964, DEF 15 IND–US.

37.　'Confidential Background Memorandum', attachment to memorandum by Kitchen to Rusk, 'Indian Ocean Islands', 8 October 1965, DEF 15 IND–US. See also Darby, *East of Suez*, pp. 265–6; and Monoranjan Bezboruah, *U.S. Strategy in the Indian Ocean: The International Response* (London and New York: Praeger, 1977) pp. 21, 60–3.

38.　See note 5 above.

39.　Department of State to US Embassies in Dar-Es-Salaam, Nairobi, Tananarive, New Delhi, Karachi and Colombo, 18 June 1964, DEF 15 IND–US.

40.　US Embassy, New Delhi, to Department of State, 14 November 1963, DDRS, 1976, 74A; US Embassy, New Delhi, to Department of State, 6 December 1963, DDRS, 1976, 74C; Department of State to US Embassy, New Delhi, 13 December, DDRS, 1976, 64F (quote).

41.　US Embassy, New Delhi, to Department of State, 17 December 1963, DDRS, 1976, 75B (quote); US Embassy, New Delhi, to Department of State, 18 December 1963, DDRS, 1976, 75F.

42.　Department of State to US Embassy, New Delhi, 24 December 1963, DDRS, 1976, 75G.

43.　Memorandum by Kitchen to Rusk, 'Discussions with the British on Indian Ocean Islands and Related Topics', 11 February 1964; Department of State to US Embassies in Dar-Es-Salaam, Nairobi, Tananarive, New Delhi, Karachi and Colombo, 18 June 1964 (quote); Department of State to US Embassy, London, 22 June 1964, both in DEF 15 IND–US.

44.　Department of State to US Embassy, London, 15 June 1964, DEF 15 IND–US.

45.　Ibid.

46.　Department of State to US Embassy, London, 3 September 1964; Kitchen to William E. Lang (Deputy Assistant Secretary of Defense for International Security Affairs), 5 November 1964 (quote), both in DEF 15 IND–US. The *Washington Post* article appeared on 29 August and the *Cleveland Plain Dealer* piece on 30 August.

47.　Memorandum by Kitchen to Ball, Harriman and Sloan, 'Discussions with the British on Indian Ocean Islands and related topics', 14 February 1964 (quote); memorandum by C. Arnold Freshman to Kitchen, 'Indian Ocean Bases', 13 August 1964, both in DEF IND–US.

48. Department of State to US Embassy, London, 22 June 1964, DEF 15 IND–UK; memorandum by Kitchen to Rusk, 'Indian Ocean Islands', 8 October 1965; Department of State to US Embassy, London, 10 November 1966, both in DEF 15 IND–UK.

49. Kitchen to Rusk, 8 October 1965, above.

50. 'Confidential Background Memorandum', attachment to Kitchen to Rusk, 8 October 1965, above; Department of State to US Embassy, London, 10 November 1966; memorandum by Joseph J. Wolf to Foy Kohler, 'BIOT', 7 December 1966, all in DEF 15 IND–US.

51. The Navy position is summarised in memorandum by Alain Enthoven, Assistant Secretary of Defense (Systems Analysis), 'Austere Support Facility on Diego Garcia', 24 October 1967, Sec Def Cont Nr. X–6590.

52. Memorandum by the Joint Chiefs of Staff to McNamara, 'Proposed Naval Facility on Diego Garcia', 25 July 1965, JCSM–420–67.

53. The Systems Analysis arguments were spelled out in the memorandum signed by Enthoven, note 31 above. McNamara's decision was communicated in McNamara to Secretary of the Navy 27 October 1967, Sec Def Cont Nr. X–6590.

54. US Congress, House Subcommittee on the Near East and South Asia, Committee on Foreign Affairs, *Proposed Expansion of U.S. Military Facilities in the Indian Ocean*, 93rd Congress, 2nd session, 1974, pp. 82–3.

55. The full story of the depopulation was related in an article, 'Diego Garcia, the Islanders Britain Sold', published in *The Sunday Times* (London) 21 September 1976 and reprinted in US Congress, House Special Subcommittee on Investigations, Committee on International Relations, *Diego Garcia, 1975: The Debate Over the Base and the Island's Former Inhabitants*, 94th Congress, 1st session, 1975, pp. 93–101.

56. Department of State to US Embassy, Cairo, 5 June 1964, DDRS, 1976, 275G.

4 Nixon and His Doctrine

1. US Congress, House Subcommittee on the Near East, Committee on Foreign Affairs, *U.S. Interests in and Policy Toward the Persian Gulf*, 92nd Congress, 2nd session, 1972, p. 95.

2. Richard M. Nixon, *U.S. Foreign Policy for the 1970's. A New Strategy for Peace*, report to the Congress, 18 February 1970, p. 6.

3. Richard M. Nixon, *U.S. Foreign Policy for the 1970's, Building for Peace*, report to the Congress, 25 February 1971, p. 14.

4. Richard M. Nixon, *U.S. Foreign Policy for the 1970's. The Emerging Structure of Peace*, report to the Congress, 9 February 1972, p. 153; Nixon, *U.S. Foreign Policy for the 1970's. Shaping a Durable Peace*, report to the Congress, 3 May 1973, p. 39; memorandum by Henry

Kissinger, 'Soviet and Friendly Naval Involvement in the Indian Ocean Area, 1971–1975', 9 November 1970, National Security Study Memorandum 104; memorandum by Kissinger, 'Follow-on Study of Strategy Toward Indian Ocean', 22 December 1970, National Security Study Memorandum 110. For a good summary of the conclusions of the Persian Gulf and Indian Ocean studies, and of the reasoning which went into them, see the July 1971 Congressional testimony by Ronald Spiers (director, State Department bureau of politico-military affairs) and Robert Pranger (Deputy Assistant Secretary of Defense, International Security Affairs, for Policy Plans and National Security Council Affairs) in US Congress, House Subcommittee on National Security Policy and Scientific Developments, Committee on Foreign Affairs, *The Indian Ocean: Political and Strategic Future*, 92nd Congress, 1st session, 1971, pp. 161–94. For the best secondary treatment of US policy in the Nixon years, written with first hand knowledge, see Gary Sick, 'The Evolution of U.S. Strategy Toward the Indian Ocean and Persian Gulf Regions', in Alvin Z. Rubinstein (ed.), *The Great Game: Rivalry in the Persian Gulf and South Asia* (New York: Praeger, 1983).

5.   The words are those of Joseph Sisco, Under Secretary of State for Political Affairs. See US Congress, House Special Subcommittee on Investigations, Committee on International Relations, *The Persian Gulf, 1975: the Continuing Debate on Arms Sales*, 94th Congress, 1st session, 1975, p. 6.

6.   See statement of James H. Noyes, Deputy Assistant Secretary of Defense (ISA) for Near Eastern, African, and South Asian Affairs, in US Congress, House Subcommitte on the Near East and South Asia, Committee on Foreign Affairs, *New Perspectives on the Persian Gulf*, 93rd Congress, 1st session, 1973, p. 39; see also US Congress, House Subcommittee on the Near East and South Asia, Committee on Foreign Affairs, *The Persian Gulf, 1974: Money, Politics, Arms, and Power*, 93rd Congress, 2nd session, 1974, p. 73.

7.   See statement of Alfred L. Atherton, Jr., Assistant Secretary of State for Near Eastern and South Asia Affairs, in US Congress, *The Persian Gulf*, 1974, p. 73.

8.   Amin Saikal, *The Rise and Fall of the Shah* (Princeton University Press, 1980), p. 140.

9.   Ibid., pp. 146–7.

10.   Ibid., pp. 138–47.

11.   Saikal, *The Rise and Fall of the Shah*, pp. 154–61; Andrew J. Pierre, *The Global Politics of Arms Sales* (Princeton University Press, 1982) pp. 142–54.

12.   Saikal, *The Rise and Fall of the Shah*, pp. 176–81.

13.   US, Department of Defense, Security Assistance Agency, *Foreign Military Sales and Military Assistance Facts*, December 1980, pp. 1–2.

14.   US, Congress, House Committee on International Relations, *United States Arms Policies in the Persian Gulf and Red Sea Areas: Past, Present, and Future*, Report of a Staff Survey Mission to Ethiopia, Iran, and the Arabian Peninsula, 95th Congress, 1st session, 1977, pp. 134–5; Henry Kissinger, *White House Years* (Boston and Toronto: Little,

Brown, 1979) p. 1264; Pierre, *Global Arms Sales*, p. 145; *New York Times*, 25 July 1971, pp. 2, 3.

15.   David M. Abshire (Assistant Secretary for Congressional Relations) to Lee H. Hamilton (D–Ind), 17 December 1971, printed in US, Congress, *U.S. Interests in and Policy Toward the Persian Gulf*, pp. 153–4.

16.   The administration position is stated in US, Congress, House Special Subcommittee on Investigations, Committee on International Relations, *The Persian Gulf, 1975: The Continuing Debate on Arms Sales*, 94th Congress, 1st session, 1975, p. 96.

17.   Ibid., p. 27; also Kissinger, *White House Years*, p. 1264.

18.   US, Congress, House Committee on International Relations, *United States Arms Policies in the Persian Gulf*, pp. 26–45; Pierre, *Global Arms Sales*, pp. 175–88.

19.   US, Department of Defense, Security Assistance Agency, *Foreign Military Sales and Military Assistance Facts*, December 1980, pp. 1–2.

20.   Pierre, *Global Arms Sales*, p. 182.

21.   US, Congress, House Committee on International Relations, *United States Arms Policies in the Persian Gulf*, pp. 76–8, 131.

22.   Pierre, *Global Arms Sales*, p. 187; Marie-Christine Aulas, 'La Diplomatique Saoudienne à L'Épreuve', *Le Monde Diplomatique*, April 1977, pp. 2–3, George Lenczowski, *The Middle East in World Affairs* (Ithaca: Cornell University Press, 1980), pp. 649–50.

23.   In 1971, three exercises were conducted in Indian Ocean waters – in April, a six-ship anti-submarine warfare exercise in the eastern Indian Ocean near Australia; in July, a non-stop transit from Singapore to Australia via the Seychelles by the nuclear-powered frigate *Truxton*; and in September, an exercise involving the nuclear-powered aircraft carrier *Enterprise* (at that time the only operational nuclear carrier) and the nuclear frigate *Bainbridge* in the eastern Indian Ocean around Indonesia. Finally, in December 1971, a carrier task force led by the *Enterprise* was sent into the Bay of Bengal as evidence of the US 'tilt' toward Pakistan during the Indo–Pakistani War. US, Congress, *U.S. Interests in and Policy toward the Persian Gulf*, p. 111.

24.   *New York Times*, 30 September 1971, p. 9; *New York Times*, 11 October 1971, p. 1; *New York Times*, 4 November 1971, p. 4; *New York Times*, 8 January 1972, p. 10.

25.   *New York Times*, 3 April 1969, p. 34; *New York Times*, 23 August 1969, p. 1; *New York Times*, 22 August 1970, p. 4; *New York Times*, 27 September 1971, p. 16; *New York Times*, 11 October 1971, p. 1.

26.   Sick, 'Evolution of U.S. Strategy', pp. 57–62; Elmo Zumwalt, *On Watch* (New York: Quadrangle/The New York Times Book Company, 1976) pp. 360–3 (quote on p. 363); *New York Times*, 28 November 1970, p. 2.

27.   Sick, 'Evolution of U.S. Strategy', pp. 63–4.

28.   Ibid.; Stephen S. Roberts, 'The October 1973 Arab–Israeli War', in Bradford Dismukes and James McConnell (eds), *Soviet Naval Diplomacy* (New York: Pergamon Press, 1979), p. 207; *New York Times*, 1 December 1973, p. 5; US, Congress, House Subcommittee on the Near East and South Asia, Committee on Foreign Affairs, *Proposed*

Expansion of U.S. Military Facilities in the Indian Ocean, 93rd Congress, 2nd session, 1974, p. 25.

29. US, Congress, *Proposed Expansion*, pp. 151, 167; US, Congress, Senate Committee on Armed Services, *Selected Material on Diego Garcia*, 94th Congress, 1st session, 1975, pp. 4–5; US, Congress, House Special Subcommittee on Investigations, Committee on International Relations, *Diego Garcia, 1975: The Debate over the Base and the Island's Former Inhabitants*, 94th Congress, 1st session, 1975, p. 7; US, Congress, Senate Committee on Armed Services, *Military Construction Authorization, FY 1975*, Senate Report 93–1136 accompanying HR 16136, 93rd Congress, 2nd session, 1974, p. 7; *Congressional Record*, 94th Congress, 1st session, 6 November 1975, 121: 35340–54. The administration had been rebuffed in initial attempts to fund the logistical facility approved by Clark Clifford in 1968. In Fiscal Year 1970 (calendar year 1969), the Navy approached Congress with a request for the first increment of construction money to build the base. The House and Senate Armed Services Committees and the House Appropriations Military Construction Subcommittee approved the proposal, but the Senate refused to follow suit. Richard B. Russell, powerful chairman of the Senate Appropriations Committee, opposed the base, as did members of the Subcommittee on Military Construction. A compromise was reached in conference: the Navy would present another proposal in Fiscal Year 1971 for money to construct a communications facility; all funds for the support facility would be deleted. Accordingly, in Fiscal Year 1971, the Congress authorised $20.45 million for building a 'limited communications station' on Diego Garcia; $5.4 million was appropriated to start work. Since none of the policy reviews of 1969 and 1970 posited need for an expanded base, the matter was let drop over the next several years.

30. US, Congress, *Proposed Expansion*, pp. 167–8; James R. Schlesinger to John C. Stennis (Chairman, Senate Armed Services Committee) 16 February 1974, printed in US, Congress, *Selected Material on Diego Garcia*, pp. 12–13 (quote); US, Congress, Senate Subcommittee on Military Construction, *Second Supplemental Appropriations for Fiscal Year 1974*, pp. 2115, 2138, 2140–2; US, Congress, House Subcommittee on Military Construction, *Second Supplemental Appropriations Bill, FY 1974*, p. 55. Administration spokesmen played down strategic options the base might afford in the Indian Ocean littoral. In their words, it would 'provide support for a flexible range of activities, including maintenance, bunkering, aircraft staging, and enhanced communications', relieving the 'strain' of supporting naval operations thousands of miles from the nearest base. It would be 'a super filling station' where the fleet could pick up the 'windshield wipers, and the tires, and whatnot that a filling station provides'. Why the fleet might need this filling station was not specified in great detail. Nor was the meaning of the phrase 'aircraft staging'. *Without* an expanded runway, the base was able to accommodate *all* Navy and Air Force aircraft but the KC–135 tanker and the B–52 bomber. *With* the 4000 foot extension (from 8000 to 12 000 feet) it could accommodate the KC–135 tanker –

which could refuel B–52s. The expense of the purported filling station was understated along with the uses. The FY 1974 supplemental budget contained $29 million to fund construction; further costs would add (supposedly) $8.3 million to the final bill. Under Congressional prodding, however, the fact emerged that the total planned expenditure was really $137.2 million: the Navy had neglected to mention the salaries of Seabees who were building the base or the cost of communications equipment and other machinery which would be installed there. See US, Congress, *Proposed Expansion*, pp. 54, 167–8; US, Congress, House Subcommittee on Military Construction, Committee on Appropriations, *Second Supplemental Appropriations Bill, FY 1974*, part 1, 93rd Congress, 2nd session, 1974, pp. 61, 74–5, 78; US, Congress, *Diego Garcia, 1975*, pp. 8–9, 28–9.

31. US, Congress, *The Indian Ocean: Political and Strategic Future*, p. 176.
32. US, Congress, *U.S. Interests in and Policy toward the Persian Gulf*, p. 2.
33. US, Congress, Senate Subcommittee on Military Appropriations, *Second Supplemental Appropriations for Fiscal Year 1974*, pp. 2119.
34. US, Congress, *Proposed Expansion*, p. 34.
35. Ibid., pp. 27–8.
36. Henry Kissinger, *Years of Upheaval* (Boston: Little, Brown, 1982), p. 625.
37. Ibid., p. 1036.
38. Ibid., p. 626.
39. Ibid.
40. See statement in Kissinger news conference at Jerusalem, 17 June 1974, in *The Department of State Bulletin* 71, 1829 (15 July 1974): 125.
41. In his 17 September news conference in Cincinnati, Kissinger declared, 'The U.S. preference prior to Rabat had been that the issue should be settled in negotiation between Jordan and Israel. That was the position we supported, and that is still basically our preference.' *The Department of State Bulletin* 73, 1893 (6 October 1975): 510.
42. Ibid.
43. These documents are printed in US, Congress, House Committee on Foreign Affairs, *The Search for Peace in the Middle East, 1967–79*, pp. 93, 97, 101.
44. US, Department of Defense, Security Assistance Agency, *Foreign Military Sales and Military Assistance Facts*, September 1983, p. 10.

5 Carter Closes the Clasp

1. The words are from an October 1976 memorandum prepared by Cyrus Vance setting out the goals and priorities of Carter's foreign policy should he be elected. Printed in Cyrus Vance, *Hard Choices* (New York: Simon and Schuster, 1983) p. 441.
2. Ibid., p. 163.
3. Zbigniew Brzezinski, *Power and Principle: Memoirs of the National Security Adviser, 1977–1981* (New York: Farrar, Straus, Giroux, 1983) p. 83.
4. Vance, *Hard Choices*, p. 164.

5. Brzezinski, *Power and Principle*, pp. 84–6. Brzezinski reproduces the conclusions of the Brookings study on pp. 85–6.
6. *Department of State Bulletin*, 77, 1998 (10 October 1977): 463.
7. The text of the statement is reproduced in Vance, *Hard Choices*, pp. 463–4.
8. Ibid., p. 194.
9. Brzezinski, *Power and Principle*, p. 112.
10. Vance, pp. 197–8; Brzezinski, *Power and Principle*, p. 113.
11. Brzezinski, *Power and Principle*, p. 244.
12. Vance, *Hard Choices*, p. 223.
13. *Public Papers of the Presidents: Jimmy Carter, 1979*: 517. For the texts of the Camp David 'peace frameworks' and of the Egyptian–Israeli treaty, see US, Congress, *The Search for Peace in the Middle East: Documents and Statements*, 1976–79, 96th Congress, 1st session, pp. 20–90.
14. Brzezinski, *Power and Principle*, p. 274.
15. Ibid., p. 273; Vance, *Hard Choices*, pp. 225, 228.
16. *Public Papers of the Presidents: Jimmy Carter, 1977*: 2173 (quote); *New York Times*, 8 January 1978, pp. 1, 7.
17. Brzezinski, *Power and Principle*, p. 438; Vance, *Hard Choices*, pp. 253–5.
18. *Public Papers of the Presidents: Jimmy Carter, 1977* (Washington: USGPO, 1978): 2031. For figures on US arms transfers to friendly governments, see US, Department of Defense, Security Assistance Agency, *Foreign Military Sales and Military Assistance Facts*, December 1980, pp. 1–12. The most controversial of the early Carter proposals was the so-called 'package deal', announced on 14 February 1978, whereby 4.8 billion dollars' worth of military aircraft would be sold to Israel, Saudi Arabia and Egypt. Under it, Israel would receive 15 F–15s and 75 F–16s; Saudi Arabia would purchase 60 F–15s; and Egypt would receive 50 F–5Es, paid for by the Saudis. The Administration made it clear that the package would have to stand as a whole: if one part of it were rejected by Congress, then all parts would be cancelled. The proposal was ratified by Congress despite strenuous opposition from the pro-Israel lobby.
19. For a full treatment of the naval arms control talks, see William Stivers, 'Doves, Hawks, and Detente', *Foreign Policy* 45, Winter 1981–2, pp. 126–44.
20. *New York Times*, 6 January 1978, pp. A1, A4.
21. Harold Brown, *Department of Defense Annual Report, Fiscal Year 1979*, 2 February 1978, p. 1.
22. Ibid., p. 16.
23. Ibid., p. 8.
24. In his testimony before the House Budget Committee on 1 October 1980, RDJTF commander General P.X. Kelley noted that with 'the emphasis at the time being focused primarily on bolstering NATO, the creation of such a force was quite logically placed on the back burner.' US, Congress, House Committee on the Budget, *Military Readiness and the Rapid Deployment Joint Task Force (RDJTF)*, 96th Congress, 2nd session, 1980, p. 45.

25. US, Congress, House Subcommittee on Europe and the Middle East, Committee on Foreign Affairs, *U.S. Interests in, and Policies toward, the Persian Gulf, 1980*, 96th Congress, 2nd session, 1980, pp. 111–18.
26. Pierre, *Global Arms Sales*, pp. 187–8; Sick, 'Evolution of U.S. Strategy', pp. 70–1; *New York Times*, 11 March 1979, p. E2;
27. Sick, 'Evolution of U.S. Strategy', p. 72.
28. Memorandum prepared in the Office of the Assistant Secretary of Defense (Program Analysis and Evaluation), 'Capabilities for Limited Contingencies in the Persian Gulf', (hereafter cited as 'Wolfowitz Report') 15 June 1979, p. 2.
29. *New York Times*, 2 October 1979, p. 18.
30. US, Library of Congress, Congressional Reference Service, *Rapid Deployment Force*, Issue Brief Number IB80027, 9 September 1982, p. 1; Sick, 'Evolution of U.S. Strategy', p. 72. US, Congress, Senate Committee on Armed Services, *Department of Defense Authorization for Appropriations for Fiscal Year 1981*, Part 1, 96th Congress, 2nd session, 1980, p. 476. US, Congress, House Subcommittee on Military Construction Appropriations, Committee on Appropriations, *Military Construction Appropriations for 1981*, 96th Congress, 2nd session, p. 1217.
31. Wolfowitz Report, p. I–1.
32. *Public Papers of the Presidents: Jimmy Carter, 1980–81*: p. 22.
33. Ibid., pp. 196–7.
34. House Subcommittee on Europe and the Middle East, *Persian Gulf, 1980*, pp. 94–5; House Committee on the Budget, *Rapid Deployment Joint Task Force*, pp. 45–7.
35. Harold Brown, *Department of Defense Annual Report, Fiscal Year 1981*, pp. 11, 209–14; Congressional Reference Service, *Rapid Deployment Force*, p. 12; Congressional Reference Service, *Defense Budget – FY 1983: Strategic Mobility (Airlift and Sealift)*, Issue Brief Number IB82035, 10 September 1982.
36. Senate Committee on Armed Services, *Department of Defense Authorization for Fiscal Year 1981*, p. 498; House Subcommittee on Europe and the Middle East, *Persian Gulf, 1980*, p. 65.
37. US, Congress, House Subcommittee on Military Construction Appropriations, Committee on Appropriations, *Military Construction Appropriations for 1981*, 96th Congress, 2nd session, p. 1061; *Washington Post*, 7 August 1980, p. A1.
38. *Washington Post*, 2 February 1980, p. A1.
39. Sick, 'Evolution of U.S. Strategy', pp. 74–5; Senate Committee on Armed Services, *Department of Defense Authorization . . . for Fiscal Year 1981*, p. 435; *Washington Post*, 7 August 1980, p. A1; *Washington Post*, 10 August 1980, p. A1; *New York Times*, 27 August 1980, p. 2; *New York Times*, 12 November 1980, pp. 6, 7; *New York Times*, 21 November 1980, p. 18; Pierre, *Global Arms Sales*, p. 169.
40. For an extensive treatment of the Camp David negotiations see Seth Tillman, *The United States in the Middle East* (Bloomington: University of Indiana Press, 1982), esp. pp. 111–12, 206–9.

41. Pierre, *Global Arms Sales*, pp. 168–9; *New York Times*, 26 February 1980, p. 8. Touting his own capabilities in May 1980, Sadat exclaimed, 'I can raise a million-soldier army. I have my pilots that have astonished American officials on the Phantom. . . . Send me war gear.' *Washington Post*, 26 May 1980, p. A20.
42. Sick, 'Evolution of U.S. Strategy', p. 75.
43. *New York Times*, 10 January 1980, p. 18; *New York Times*, 30 March 1980, pp. 1, 9.
44. Harold Brown, *Annual Report, FY 1981*, p. 30.
45. Ibid., pp. 61–2.
46. *Washington Post*, 2 February 1980, p. A1; 10 August 1980, pp. A1, 12.
47. Senate Committee on Armed Services, *Department of Defense Authorization . . . for Fiscal Year 1981*, p. 445. The Wolfowitz Report conveyed the same conclusion: 'Although the most extreme military threat to Western interests in the Persian Gulf would probably be a Soviet invasion of Iran, other contingencies are more likely and more immediately threatening. Local insurgencies and conflicts may not only endanger governments friendly to the West, but may also threaten the physical flow of oil through destruction of facilities and labour disruptions.' Wolfowitz Report, p. III–1.
48. House Subcommittee on Europe and the Middle East, *Persian Gulf, 1980*, p. 4.
49. See Komer testimony, ibid., pp. 81–2.
50. See, for example, Saunders testimony in House Subcommittee on Europe and the Middle East, *Persian Gulf, 1980*, p. 3. See also Wolfowitz Report, p. I–5.
51. Wolfowitz Report, p. 2.

6 Reagan Takes Charge

1. 'Face the Nation' interview, CBS television network, 8 March 1981.
2. Caspar Weinberger, *Department of Defense Annual Report, Fiscal Year 1983*, 8 February 1982, p. II–3.
3. US, Congress, Senate Armed Services Committee, *Department of Defense Authorization for Appropriations for Fiscal Year 1982*, 97th Congress, 1st session, part 4, p. 1714; US, Congress, Senate Armed Services Committee, *Department of Defense Authorization for Appropriations for Fiscal Year 1983*, 97th Congress, 2nd session, part 6, p. 3768.
4. Senate Armed Services Committee, *Department of Defense Authorization, FY 1983*, part 6, p. 3732.
5. Weinberger, *Department of Defense Annual Report, Fiscal Year 1984*, 1 February 1983, p. 37.
6. *New York Times*, 30 May 1982, pp. 1, 12; *New York Times*, 25 October 1982, pp. A1, A14 (quote).
7. *Public Papers of the Presidents of the United States: Ronald Reagan, 1981* (Washington: USGPO, 1978): 871.
8. *Public Papers of the Presidents; Ronald Reagan, 1981*: 952.
9. Senate Armed Services Committee, *Department of Defense Authoriza-*

tion, FY 1982, part 1, p. 15 (quote); Senate Armed Services Committee, *Department of Defense Authorization, FY 1982*, part 4, p. 1701.

10. US, Congress, House Subcommittee on Military Construction, Committee on Appropriations, *Military Construction Appropriations for 1982*, 97th Congress, 1st session, part 6, pp. 243–4; *New York Times*, 24 April 1981, p. 3; *New York Times*, 4 June 1981, p. 5.

11. Weinberger, *Annual Report, FY 1984*, pp. 198 (quote), 199; US, Congress, Congressional Budget Office, *Rapid Deployment Forces: Policy and Budgetary Implications*, February 1983, p. xv; *New York Times*, 30 April 1982, p. A3; *New York Times*, 25 October 1982, pp. A1, A14.

12. Senate Armed Services Committee, *Department of Defense Authorization, FY 1982*, part 1, p. 17.

13. Senate Armed Services Committee, *Department of Defense Authorization, FY 1983*, part 6, p. 3717.

14. See note 12 above.

15. Weinberger, *Department of Defense Annual Report, FY 1983*, pp. I–16.

16. *New York Times*, 20 March 1981, p. A1.

17. *New York Times*, 23 February 1981, pp. A1, A5; *New York Times*, 3 March 1981, p. A8.

18. *Wall Street Journal*, 3 June 1980, pp. 1, 25.

19. Senate Armed Services Committee, *Department of Defense Authorization, FY 1982*, part 4, p. 1713.

20. Ibid., p. 1719. In his interview on the CBS 'Face the Nation' programme on 8 March 1981, Weinberger declared: 'I think it is essential that we have a presence in the Middle East, or Southwest Asia, as it seems to be called more and more now. I think that if we have two things – if we have some facilities and additional men and material either placed there or nearby, it will act as a deterrent to the Soviets for any more adventures coming in through Iran and Iraq and attempts to seize the oil fields.'

21. *New York Times*, 11 November 1981, p. A9; *New York Times*, 8 February 1982, p. A13.

22. For text of the agreement, see US, Congress, House Subcommittee on Europe and the Middle East, Committee on Foreign Affairs, *Documents and Statements on Middle East Peace, 1979–82*, 97th Congress, 2nd session, p. 256.

23. Ibid., p. 257.

24. Enver M. Koury, 'The Impact of the Geopolitical Situation of Iraq on the Gulf Cooperation Council', *Middle East Insight*, 2, 5 (January/February 1983), pp. 28–35; *New York Times*, 23 February 1981, p. A6; *New York Times*, 6 November 1981, p. A4; *New York Times*, 11 November 1981, p. A9; Senate Armed Services Committee, *Department of Defense Authorization, FY 1982*, part 1, p. 371.

25. *New York Times*, 9 March 1981, p. A3; House Appropriations Committee, *Military Construction, FY 1982*, part 6, pp. 228–9; Senate Armed Services Committee, *Department of Defense Authorization, FY 1983*, part 6, pp. 3743, 3765.

26. *Washington Post*, 21 May 1983, p. A18; *Middle East International*, 24 June 1983, p. 8.
27. Speech printed in *New York Times*, 27 May 1982, p. A10.
28. Hedrick Smith, 'White House Shifting Mideast Stand', *New York Times*, 29 May 1982, p. A8.
29. Zeev Schiff, 'Green Light, Lebanon', *Foreign Policy*, 50 (Spring 1983): 73–85.
30. *New York Times*, 8 June 1982, pp. A1, A14 (quote), A15; *New York Times*, 12 June 1982, pp. A1, A5.
31. Barry Rubin, 'The Reagan Administration and the Middle East', in *Eagle Defiant: United States Foreign Policy in the 1980s*, ed. Kenneth Oye, Robert Lieber and Donald Rothchild (Boston: Little, Brown, 1983) pp. 377–8.
32. US Congress, Senate Foreign Relations Committee, *Nomination of George P. Shultz*, 97th Congress, 2nd Sess., p. 11.
33. Printed in *Weekly Compilation of Presidential Documents*, 18, 35 (6 September 1982): 1081–5.
34. 'Face the Nation' interview, CBS television network, 5 September 1982.
35. *Washington Post*, 23 September 1982, pp. A1, A40–1.
36. *Washington Post*, 21 September 1982, pp. A1, A13.
37. *Washington Post*, 24 September 1982, pp. A1, A19 (quote).
38. The text of the agreement is printed in *New York Times*, 17 May 1983, p. A12. See also *New York Times*, 10 May 1983, pp. A1, A8.
39. *New York Times*, 7 May 1983, pp. A1, A4; *New York Times*, pp. A1, A5; *Washington Post*, 20 May 1983, pp. A1, A22.

Index